Crying Baby,
Sleepless Nights

Crying Baby, Sleepless Nights

SANDY JONES

THE HARVARD COMMON PRESS
Harvard and Boston, Massachusetts

The Harvard Common Press
535 Albany Street
Boston, Massachusetts 02118

Printed in the United States of America.

Library of Congress Cataloging-in-Publication Data

Jones, Sandy.
    Crying baby, sleepless nights : why your baby is crying and
what you can do about it / by Sandy Jones. — Rev. ed.
      p.   cm.
    Includes bibliographical references and index.
    ISBN 1-55832-046-6 (cloth)
    ISBN 1-55832-045-8 (paper)
    1. Infants (Newborn)—Care. 2. Crying in infants.
    I. Title.
RJ253.J66 1992
649.122—dc20   92-10441

Cover design by Joyce Weston

10 9 8 7 6 5 4 3 2 1

CONTENTS

FOREWORD

Several years ago a West Coast diaper service surveyed its customers on their feelings about parenting. What did they feel was the hardest thing about being a new parent? "Lack of sleep," was one of the most common replies. Adjusting to parenthood can be doubly difficult when you are tired all the time. Yet most infants will wake up at night and go through some fussy periods. So what's a parent to do?

In the news lately have been a lot of "experts" who offer system-ized approaches to solving the problem of fussy, wakeful babies. Their methods usually come down to letting the baby cry it out until he stops from exhaustion or gives up in despair that anyone lis-tening to him really cares.

I remember meeting a young couple who had used this technique quite successfully. Their eleven-month-old daughter had been sleep-ing through the night for months. But their problem was the uproar she caused when they tried to get her ready for bed. She fought them tooth and nail to keep from being put down. "How lucky you are," I told the couple, "to have a daughter so persistent in fighting for her needs. She's not given up trying to tell you how much she needs to be near you at night." Letting a baby cry it out is a short-term solu-tion whose long-term ramifications are not in the best interest of either baby or parents.

When a popular newspaper columnist was asked how to handle a ten-month-old's night waking her advice was similar. The parent should go to the baby and check that everything is all right, then gently pat him on the back, say "I love you," and firmly walk out the door. Can't you just see the wife of that baby, thirty years from now, seeking help for her marriage because, while her husband professes to love her, he's never around when she really needs him!

The advice was similar when my own children were small. We were told that if your baby stopped crying when you picked him up then you knew he just wanted to be held, so you could put him back down with a clear conscience. This perspective totally ignored a baby's need to be with its mother, reassured by her presence—a need that serves as a survival mechanism.

Some babies need physical closeness more than others. Philip, the youngest of our seven children, is a good example. He literally lived on my body for the first three months of his life. He would awaken immediately if he was put down to sleep. So I got hold of a Mexican rebozo, a long rectangular piece of woven cloth. The rebozo went across my shoulders and around Philip, holding him close to my body while leaving my arms free. I was amused eighteen years later, when Philip returned from three weeks in the Rocky Mountains on an Outward Bound survival expedition, to learn that his favorite part of that challenging experience was the "solo," the three days he spent *alone* in the wilderness.

Raising a baby, it seems to me, involves trust and unconditional love as much as the specifics of care and feeding. In fact, all these things go together. The intensity of our full-time involvement during the period babies are so dependent gives us an unequaled opportunity to stretch and grow. Caring for a baby can be likened to the total-immersion techniques used to teach languages and other skills. And, like foreign-language students, we learn most effectively when we have a skilled and sensitive facilitator.

In *Crying Baby, Sleepless Nights*, Sandy Jones has set out to be that facilitator—to provide direction and understanding to parents. If I were to add anything to this most comprehensive book it would be a bit more emphasis on taking advantage of help from family and friends and groups like La Leche League, and a clear appreciation of how much our attitudes can help us to handle stress.

When our daughter Melanie had unexpected twins after her first pregnancy, the whole family shifted gears to be available. Sometimes the calmer heartbeat of a helper, we found, could make all the difference in settling a fussy baby down. It was often my husband, Tom, with his deep, resonant voice, who was most successful at getting a baby to sleep while doing his "grand" parent dance. As the twins got older their father found that playing the harmonica with a baby on his shoulder was another successful sleep inducer.

Accepting that we might not get a full night's sleep for a while is in itself a stress reliever. It was clear that our daughter Laurel had unconsciously made things easy on herself when she excitedly announced that her son, Austin, was already sleeping through the night at three months. Yes, it was really true, she went on to explain: Austin, who sleeps with his parents, "gets up to nurse two or three times a night, goes right back to sleep, *and sleeps all night long!*"

Way back when I was born, babies were fed on four-hour schedules, and mothers were told not to pick up their babies in between. Many of my mother's friends have told me of standing by their baby's bedside—the baby crying, the mother crying—watching the clock for permission to pick the baby up. But my maternal grandmother, after whom I was named, gave me a priceless gift when she spoke up, insisting to my parents that it was wrong to leave a baby alone to cry. And so, being a colicky breastfed baby, I was held constantly and even slept with my parents for the first year of my life.

"Crying," Dr. Lee Salk said many times, "is as good for the lungs as bleeding is for the veins." Deciphering and answering a baby's cries can teach us a lot about the baby's uniqueness and can bring out the best in ourselves. And isn't that all part of what parenting is about?

MARIAN TOMPSON
Cofounder and President Emeritus
La Leche League International

PREFACE

As a veteran parent, I understand how stressful and exhausting caring for a baby can be. I've journeyed all the way through adolescence with my daughter, Marcie, who never slept more than three hours at a time in her first two years. I can still remember sitting in the bathroom doorway, feeling worn out and unsupported as I tried to let Marcie cry it out. I feel sad for myself now, when I remember how lonely and isolated I felt then. In part, *Crying Baby, Sleepless Nights* was born of my wish that other parents never have to feel as alone as I did when they are faced with a baby's fussy wakefulness.

I have learned a lot since the first edition of *Crying Baby, Sleepless Nights* was published in 1983. Besides carefully reviewing over a thousand medical, psychiatric, and psychological studies of infants, I have traveled nationwide to talk with hundreds of parents of fussy babies. I've shared their frustrations, their worries, their loneliness, their despair.

For a year and a half, I worked with a group of low-income, inner-city teenage mothers and their babies. I learned a lot about how to help mothers with the challenges of parenting. I learned to recognize the difference between good and poor mother-baby relationships, and I learned that a mother's perception of her baby as "bad" can become a self-fulfilling prophecy.

I have also counseled hundreds of troubled adults, many of whom have suffered from deep yearnings, sadness, and hopelessness all their lives. When I've joined them in reviving their earliest memories, profoundly painful feelings have arisen from their past as babies and young children. A small, child-like voice sometimes emerges when one of these adults recalls screaming in a crib and getting no response. How terrible it is to be a baby totally dependent upon another human being who ignores your pleas for help.

But I sympathize, too, with the parents of such babies. Even the most experienced and self-confident parent feels inadequate when facing a fussy, miserable baby. Parents who are isolated, worried, and exhausted have a harder time answering all their babies' demands. They may be easily seduced by someone's latest technique to teach a baby not to cry, or to sleep through the night, in fourteen days or less. Or they may accept a doctor's offer of drugs to stop the crying, without first knowing clearly what the cause of the baby's distress is, or what harmful side effects the drugs might have.

It is a tremendous privilege to have arrived at the other end of parenting, when a child is mature and ready to leave the nest. In the early days of childrearing, it would have been a great relief to know that my baby's sleep problem would resolve itself in due time, that I would remember the nursing years with great tenderness, and that my daughter would turn out to be a bright, responsible, and sociable adult. With this book I hope to provide you with the reassurance I lacked—that love, compassion, and responsiveness really work, and are the appropriate way to treat children at every stage of their development.

Few parents of babies have hours to spend reading any book from cover to cover, so I've designed this one for people who have only five minutes a day to concentrate on anything but their fussy babies. The book contains brief, comprehensible explanations and plenty of charts to speed up your search for answers. In the margins you'll find comments from other parents about their fussy babies, and some wise words from medical researchers and practitioners on every aspect of babies' crying and sleeplessness. The last two chapters are meant to help you sustain yourself through what may well be the most challenging time in your life.

One mother told me, "If my baby is going to suffer, I don't want him to suffer alone." *Your* baby shouldn't suffer alone, and *you* shouldn't, either. May this book provide the knowledge and solace you need so you can in turn help your baby to feel pain-free, comfortable, and well-loved.

ACKNOWLEDGMENTS

I'D LIKE TO THANK REID BOATES, the editor of the first edition of *Crying Baby, Sleepless Nights*, who was prompted to ask me to write the book by his own fussy son, Joseph Scott. Joseph, who is now eleven, has happily turned out to be "an absolute prince—a scholar and an athlete and all those things a father brags about," according to Reid.

A special note of gratitude also goes to my present editor, Linda Ziedrich. Linda has made a tremendous contribution to this book through her clear insight and her own mothering experience. Some of the very practical suggestions regarding sensitive baby handling that appear in this edition have come from Linda's own experiences as a breastfeeding mother. I am deeply indebted to her for her contributions to this book.

I also wish to acknowledge the helpful suggestions from Janet Jendron, a member of La Leche League's Board of Directors and an altogether practical and caring mother. Janet contributed tremendously to this book, because she believed in it. In addition I would like to thank Kathleen Huggins, author of *The Nursing Mother's Companion*; Muriel Boette, a nurse and lactation consultant; and Richard Boette, a pediatrician who has worked with many fussy babies. All three offered valuable insights that helped me to fine-tune the text. And I thank my daughter, Marcie, who has taught me a lot of very important lessons about being a mother and a "human bean."

In my thoughts throughout this arduous updating process has been a beautiful little baby named Florence Dion, although I never met her in person. Her mother, Andrée, wrote a poignant letter telling me that she had read the first edition of *Crying Baby, Sleepless Nights* when she was pregnant and that it ingrained in her mind the idea that a baby should not be left to cry.

After she was born Florence cried a lot, her mother wrote. Andrée and her husband took turns walking their baby around their tiny apartment and singing to her night after night. It wasn't until months later that they learned Florence had a severe heart condition. If she had been left to cry, she would have died quickly. Florence finally did die, her mother told me, after several operations, none of them successful. "The seven and a half months with Florence were exhausting," Andrée wrote, "but I'm glad we forgot about sleep and took time with Florence. It was worth it."

Enclosed in the letter was the photograph of a beautiful, smiling, brown-eyed baby in her walker, her arms outstretched as if to embrace me. Florence smiled at me the whole time I worked on the book, giving me the strength to keep on day and night.

Thank you, dear baby—and *all* babies, mothers, and fathers who have taught me on my journey.

CHAPTER ONE

Baby Crying Basics

WHEN YOU HAVE A BABY, one thing's for sure—you'll hear crying, and possibly a lot of it. Crying is a baby's most powerful mode of communication. And it's important from the moment he is born. Right after birth, your baby will probably be quite blue. After a gulp, a cough, or a squeal, he will draw his first breath and then begin to cry, every cry stronger than the one before it. The high-pitched wails will last about a second, to be followed by silence while the baby struggles for more air. As oxygen flows into your baby's lungs and arteries, his body will flush a rich pink.

The first cry is a relief to everybody. It means your baby is alive and responding. It signals to you and your attendants that your baby has surmounted the first big hurdle of life—being born.

While you were pregnant, your baby got all of his needs met without even asking, but now that he's been born, he has to signal you to get what he needs. Pain, which he hardly knew in the womb, has now become a sharp, terrifying reality for him. He can't reassure himself that everything's going to be all right, as you can. He feels all discomfort—from hunger, circumcision, a heel prick, or a belly-ache—not in just one place, but all over.

Some people think crying is good for a baby. They may tell you that it makes his lungs stronger, or sends oxygen to his blood. But the real truth is that crying is hard on a baby, and it uses up his limited resources. Although young babies can't help crying, you can tell it is self-punishing behavior. When a baby's cries aren't stopped, his arms and legs tighten, his mouth gets dry, his lips start to turn blue, his lungs probably ache, his blood pressure goes up, the veins in his head may swell and even break, and his blood oxygen level starts to go down, not up.[1]

Most newborns cry very easily. They often go back and forth between lethargy and fussing. One of the main causes for a baby's crying is hunger. When he tries to suck his hand or mouths at your shoulder, he is just asking to nurse. If he has trouble latching on, or his nose gets buried in your breast, or the milk sprays out too fast, he cries harder still. A baby often takes days to establish his sucking skill, and it may take the two of you several weeks to polish the feeding process.

Even though the hospital nurses may try to convince you that you should control when your baby nurses, it is best to feed him whenever he wants. This will encourage your milk to come in sooner, and your uterus to contract back to normal.

There are other things besides hunger that make a baby cry. A baby may simply be upset and confused about finding himself in this brightly lit and gravity-heavy world. He may have a headache or other aches from the process of being born. He may startle and cry every time you jar him, or when you undress him or change his diaper. He may cry if you lower his head too quickly, or if he hears a loud noise. A newborn's startle response, or Moro reflex, makes him throw out his hands and grasp at the air with his fingers, as though he is falling and trying to hold on. After startling he'll probably take a breath, and then cry.

Newborns are upset by the crying of other babies, too. Sometimes crying storms get started in a hospital nursery when one baby cries. Then all the other babies join in, as in sympathy.

A strong, sharp pain—from a heel prick or circumcision, for instance—will elicit from a baby a special, more shrill cry, to be followed by a scarily long pause, then another scream. A baby in pain may also grimace or groan, lower and furrow his brow, and squeeze his eyes shut. He will open his mouth wide with each cry, and you can see his arched, taut tongue inside. His trunk and limbs will be tense. He may seem pale, with damp palms, and the pupils of his eyes may be dilated more than normal. He will breathe faster than usual, and his heart will beat faster. Blood tests of babies crying with pain show increased blood sugar (hyperglycemia) and higher-than-normal blood pressure.

When a young baby is subjected to a very painful procedure, such as circumcision, without being given anesthesia, he trembles, cries vigorously, and sometimes turns blue. His heart and breathing rates dramatically increase, and large shifts occur in his oxygen and hormone levels. After the procedure, he may shut down into a deep

TIPS FOR HANDLING YOUR NEWBORN

✔ If your baby is sucking his fingers or fist, he may simply be hungry. Try feeding him.

✔ Move your baby slowly to allow him time to adjust to changes in position.

✔ Talk to him in a gentle, slow voice, as though he understood exactly what you were saying. Tell him when you plan to pick him up, and ask him if it's all right before you do it.

✔ Hold him so that his face is about 8 inches from yours when you want to talk with him. This is the distance at which his eyes focus best.

✔ If your baby isn't hungry, but he's a little fussy, try putting him up to your shoulder. He may stop fussing to look around.

✔ Be alert for your baby's cues that he has had enough socializing. He may hiccup, turn his head to the side, sneeze, or begin to grimace.

✔ Most babies don't like to have their heads controlled, so don't try to force him onto your breast by pushing him on the back of his head, and be sure to stretch the neck of T-shirts before pulling them over his head.

✔ To avoid exposing your baby to sudden temperature changes, unwrap him slowly. Keep a warm blanket over him when you change his clothes or diapers, especially if the room is drafty.

✔ If your baby startles easily, wrap him firmly in a light blanket so that his arms and legs are restrained. It may help him to feel like he's back in the womb, which was home such a short while ago.

sleep, instead of fussing and crying inconsolably as a toddler might. In the shutdown phase, he is hard to awaken, and, once awake, he is irritable and hard to soothe for several days, partly from the continuing pain but partly from the trauma of the initial experience.[2] (For more on circumcision, see page 100.)

People who work all day long with groups of babies may get used to their crying and stop taking it as seriously as parents do. They can take babies' cries lightly, but you can't. The crying is not from *their* baby, and it doesn't have *their* name on it. But you know in your gut that your baby's cry is for *you.*

That babies don't cry in the hospital is a myth. Hospital nurseries are one place where babies cry a lot. In one study babies who cried almost two hours a day in the hospital nursery averaged only twenty-two to sixty-four minutes of crying after going home, probably because their parents were standing by to answer their cries. Other studies have produced parallel findings: In one, babies in a hospital nursery cried ten times as long as those who stayed with their mothers. In another, babies held during the first four hours after birth cried an average of only two minutes in that period, compared with thirty-eight minutes for babies who lay by themselves. Whereas startles were rare in babies nurtured by their mothers or close family members, according to one study, babies in the nursery startled an average of twelve times an hour. And other researchers have found that closely nurtured babies show quicker stabilization of their temperature, pulse, and respiration.[3]

A nurse who works in the newborn nursery of a large hospital describes the scene like this:

> Nurses talk across the huge room to each other. The phones are ringing at three different places. There are cold drafts from the vents. There are warmers with screaming alarms that go off every time a probe gets misplaced or the setting gets off. This is going on day and night. Neonatologists look at every baby as though it is sick, and babies get stuck too much. They are weighed on a hard, cold surface. They are bathed roughly. The lights are on high all the time, and babies get their days and nights messed up. The baby who has had a lot of things done to it is difficult for anyone to breastfeed or bottle-feed. And then there's the crying. We can have thirty babies in there at any moment. They get started crying. You can't take care of them all at once. The racket is

almost unbearable. They are left to lie there and cry until they rub their noses raw from rooting in their blankets. Babies are kept away from their mothers too much. The baby may not understand what's happening, but the baby's spirit still suffers.

This nurse encourages mothers to keep their babies in their hospital rooms, right by their sides, whenever possible. This way a mother can attune herself to her baby's signals and soothe him quickly so he doesn't learn to cry as the only way to get people's attention. A mother should show her baby from the first day out of the womb that the world is a kind, gentle, quiet place, not a loud, uncomfortable, and uncaring one.

How a Baby's Crying Affects Parents

Your baby's cry is a powerful distress signal, designed by nature so you won't ignore it. It effectively overrides all attempts at talking with anyone else. And in the face of a crying baby, your heart throbs, your blood pressure goes up, and your palms start to sweat—the same reaction you might have if you were threatened with violence or were sitting in a dentist's office waiting for a root canal.[4] These physical reactions show that while part of you is saying, "Poor little thing, I'd better go right in there and save him," another part of you is probably shouting, "Stop this noise or get me out of here!"

A baby's cry, particularly at close range, cries to be turned off. The sound averages 84 decibels when measured 10 inches from a baby's mouth. At this distance it approaches the sound level of busy street traffic, factory noise, and even the din of a riveter from 35 feet. It is 20 decibels louder than ordinary speech.

If you're breastfeeding, your baby's crying affects your body in special ways. It can make your milk let down in the middle of a shopping trip, for example. In a Finnish study, new breastfeeding mothers listened to recordings of their babies' crying while a device measured the heat of their body surface in various places. Breasts heated up quickly when the mothers heard the cries. How hot they got depended on how often a mother had heard her own baby's voice, and how many times she had breastfed him.[5] You may discover that even crying from babies you don't know can make your milk let down.

"If you're still in the hospital and your baby reacts right away to every little thing, mellow out. Turn the television off in your room. Turn down the lights. Speak softly. Change your voice. Slow down, and shut the door."

"Even young children may have the capacity to interpret and respond to nonverbal emotional expressions. . . . A toddler coming upon another child in distress will frequently cry in 'sympathy.' Apparently the information transmitted by infant vocalization is such that it can be interpreted at a very young age. Perhaps pre-speech infant vocalizations constitute a universal language that is learned quite early in life."[7]

Crying Is Complex

Infant crying is a topic that has intrigued scientists over the centuries. A hundred and sixty years ago William Gardiner published *The Music of Nature*, which described the cries of both animals and humans with musical notes. Forty years later Charles Darwin published *The Expression of the Emotions,* which explored the facial expressions of children. And forty years after that, German researchers used both musical notes and the phonetic alphabet to chart the infant cries they had captured on wax-cylinder recording devices.

Now researchers use sophisticated monitoring devices and computers to help them analyze babies' cries. One device, a sound spectrograph, records crying patterns on a continuous roll of paper. The resulting "cryprint" displays characteristics such as pitch, frequency, and the length of pauses between cries.

Cryprint patterns show that a baby's crying is complex and well-coordinated. Each baby's cry is not just one sound, but a combination of several sounds made all at once. Every baby's cry is unique—it can be identified among the cries of all other babies. And, interestingly, every sound your baby makes is a little different from every other sound he has made.

Computer models are being used to track the differences between the cries of healthy babies and those of infants with respiratory distress, bacterial meningitis, and certain metabolic disorders. In some cases a computer program has successfully pinpointed certain forms of brain damage.[6]

Scientists hope that such programs will ultimately help in diagnosing physical problems and possibly even in ascertaining a baby's future intelligence. The programs may serve as well to identify babies who are at risk for Sudden Infant Death Syndrome (SIDS), and babies who are liable to provoke abuse because of the shrill, irritating quality of their cries.

Whereas in their early days babies have little control over whether they cry or not, after the first few months they begin to learn how to make different cry sounds beyond the basic signals of hunger, rage, or pain. It's as though babies learn how to cry better over time. Using the same amount of breath, they stretch their cries into long, even wails quite unlike the uncoordinated explosive sounds of their newborn days, and they get better at using their tongues to make a variety of sounds.

The "bah-bah-bah"s that build into cries of hunger or loneliness lay the groundwork for complex human language. Babies also begin to cry in anticipation of discomfort, as well as in reaction to it. Your baby may fuss when you unbutton his top button because he knows you're going to undress him. He recognizes that his sense of security is going to be threatened by his being taken out of comfortable warmth and jostled around.[8]

Be a Good Cry Detective

Trying to figure out what your baby is signaling with his cries is like being a good detective. As you've probably already discovered, you can tell your baby's crying voice from that of other babies very quickly. One study found that a new mother could distinguish her baby's cries among those of twenty babies after listening to as little as sixteen seconds of crying—even if she had heard her baby cry only once or twice. Long separations after birth because of a forceps or cesarean delivery did not hamper a mother's ability to tell which cries belonged to her own baby.[9]

Don't feel bad, though, if you can't tell exactly what your baby is trying to say to you when he cries. Not even trained scientists using sensitive recording equipment can interpret babies' cries beyond very general classifications, such as hunger, rage, or pain. Experience helps, however, in sharpening your hunches about what's causing a baby's discomfort. A study comparing thirty-six mothers to thirty-two childless women found that the mothers could far more accurately identify different kinds of infant cries.[10]

In figuring out what their babies want, parents may consider the time of day and the baby's appearance and motions, as well as the quality of his cry. Here's how the logic might go: "If my baby's been asleep for three and a half hours and has awakened crying, he's probably hungry. If he's been up for three hours and he's batting his ear and fussing a little, he's probably ready for a nap. If he awakens in the middle of the night with a loud, piercing scream, then something's hurting him. Maybe he's got a string from his sleeper wrapped around his toe, or maybe he has an air bubble trapped in his belly and just needs to burp." After a while a parent hardly has to think through the possibilities—she just responds appropriately. You will, too.

It may be "touch and go" at first while you learn to interpret your baby's signals. And sometimes *nothing* works for long. In time you'll

QUICK REFERENCE GUIDE TO BABIES' CRYING

TYPE OF CRY	DESCRIPTION	WHAT TO DO
Hunger	Rhythmical. A short explosive cry, followed by a pause for catching the breath, then another cry. Quickly turns into a pain cry. *Extra clues*: The baby bats his cheek or ear while rooting. He may mouth his fist or suck his fingers.	*Breastfeeding:* Feed your baby whenever he wants, for as long as he wants. Allow him to finish nursing on one side before shifting him to the other (see pages 39–43). *Bottle feeding:* Let the baby establish his own feeding schedule. Check bottle nipples to see that the holes are not too small (see page 57).
Sleepiness	Less rhythmical than hunger or pain cries. Often just fussing. The baby may bat his ears, finger his hair, or alternate between sucking his fingers and crying briefly. He may look red around the eyes, and he may rub his eyes. He will turn away from adults trying to play or talk to him, and he may resist soothing attempts.	*Breastfeeding:* Retreat to a quiet, dimly lit feeding place with a rocking chair, or nurse the baby to sleep in bed. *Bottle feeding:* Hold the baby in your arms and let him fall asleep there as you feed him. Then gently lower him into bed. Resist the urge to caress the baby or play with his hair or toes while he's feeding.
Thirst	*Bottle feeding:* Same as hunger cries, but the baby is unsatisfied by formula. Thirst may be caused by excessive salt in the formula. This is normally a problem only in extremely hot weather or when the air is dry from indoor heating.	Offer the baby water that has been boiled, by the teaspoon. (Don't give too much, or the baby may lose his appetite for formula.) To increase indoor humidity, use a cold-water humidifier or an aquarium. Keep the humidifier washed out with soap and water so bacteria don't form. Keep damp towels over the heating vent or radiator, or a pan of water on the wood stove.
Stuffy nose	Because a young baby breathes only through his nose, he will wake up crying, or stop nursing to cry, if his nose is stuffed up. See chapter 7, "The Colic-Allergy Connection," and pages 110–11 on colds.	Hold the baby upright so his nasal passages can drain. Use a cold-water humidifier. Use saline solution and a rubber ear bulb-syringe to keep nasal passages clear (see pages 110–11).

QUICK REFERENCE GUIDE TO BABIES' CRYING—*Continued*

TYPE OF CRY	DESCRIPTION	WHAT TO DO
Air swallowing	Babies often swallow air during feedings. They may also swallow air during long crying bouts. *Breastfeeding:* Usually the baby feels pain immediately after feeding, though sometimes a baby awakens with a "stuck burp" as long as two hours after a meal. If milk leaks out of the side of the mouth when the baby is swallowing, he may have an incomplete seal between his mouth and the breast. Also, if the milk lets down too fast, the baby may gulp air. *Bottle feeding:* A bottle nipple that has holes too small or too large may cause excessive air to be trapped in the baby's stomach.	To test for stomach air, thump the baby lightly on his belly. If he has swallowed air, it will sound like a ripe melon. Burp the baby by either holding him against your shoulder or sitting him up and rubbing or patting his back. Keeping a baby upright in a car seat or infant seat after feeding can sometimes bring relief from stomach congestion, as can lying the baby on his right side for a few moments and then bringing him upright again. For an overactive letdown, stop nursing and wait until the spraying stops before resuming feeding.
Wet diaper	Many babies never mind wet diapers unless they have a rash, but others cry every time they urinate or soil a diaper.	If your baby hates to be wet, the diaper is the first thing to check when he starts to cry.
Internal pain	Sudden onset. The first cry is loud, long, shrill, and urgent, and is followed by a long pause as though the baby is holding his breath. Then he screams again, with a wide-open mouth and arched tongue. His chin may quiver, and his feet and hands are drawn up or cycle tensely. Possible causes of pain include an immature digestive system, gas, circumcision, muscle aches, and allergic reactions.	See chapter 7, "The Colic-Allergy Connection," and chapter 8, "Doctors, Disease, and Drugs" for discussion of the causes of pain and treatments for it.
External pain	Same cry as for internal pain. Typically the baby starts screaming suddenly for no apparent reason, often upon awakening from a sound sleep.	Crying may be caused by tight bands on clothing, scratchy diaper covers, irritating fabrics, or an open diaper pin. Check each toe and finger to see if they have become strangled by a loose string on a sleeper or blanket, or by a long hair. Pain may also be caused by urine or feces on sore, rashy skin (see pages 113–15).

Continued on next page

QUICK REFERENCE GUIDE TO BABIES' CRYING—*Continued*

TYPE OF CRY	DESCRIPTION	WHAT TO DO
Overfeeding	Frequent spitting up and discomfort soon after meals. (See pages 51–52.)	*Breastfeeding:* Allow the baby to nurse for a long time on one side, and change sides only after he releases the breast. If the baby cries less than an hour or two after a meal, try other comforting measures before feeding him again. *Bottle feeding:* Babies do not begin to regulate their own formula intake until the second month. Until then, they will drink from a bottle until it runs dry, even though they are bloated from excess fluid. If your baby spits up and fusses a lot after meals, more frequent, smaller feedings may be needed.
Fever and illness	A whiny, nasal cry very similar to the pain cry. The baby may appear either flushed or pale. His skin will feel hot. Fever may be caused by infection or a recent inoculation.	Consult your physician if the baby is under three months old, or at any age if symptoms are worrisome. Don't overdress the baby. Aspirin can be dangerous for a baby, and other fever-reducing medications may prolong the illness (see page 98).
Anger or frustration	The baby's face may have a snarled expression; his hands may be tightly fisted. He may arch his back or turn his head to the side to signal that he doesn't like something you are doing. Things that make a baby angry: your pulling the nipple from his mouth when he's trying to nurse; his losing his pacifier; uncomfortable positioning; being undressed if it's cold; and restraint of his head, such as when you hold his head while he is trying to nurse, pull a T-shirt over his head, put a hat on him, or put him in a snug head support in an infant carrier.	Observe what makes your baby cry and then change what you're doing to make him more comfortable. Examples: help your baby find his hand or finger rather than being dependent on a pacifier, keep him covered during diaper changes, and stretch T-shirts wide before pulling them over his head.

QUICK REFERENCE GUIDE TO BABIES' CRYING—*Continued*

TYPE OF CRY	DESCRIPTION	WHAT TO DO
Tension release from overstimulation	The baby cries long and hard, and is unresponsive to efforts to nurse, rock, or cuddle him. Once he's cried for a while, he may calmly settle down for nursing or sleep. This letting-off-steam cry usually comes in the evening after a long, stimulating day or overly exciting handling.	Avoid vigorous play in the late afternoon or before bedtime. Take the baby for a long walk after he has cried a while, or rock him, then lay him down and pat his back. Or put him in his car or infant seat in front of a lamp or window. *Breastfeeding:* Nurse the baby to sleep in bed. You sleep, too—you probably need rest as much as he does. *Bottle feeding:* Let the baby drink from the bottle while falling asleep in your arms, then lower him into bed.
Too cold	Babies are cold-sensitive during the first few weeks. Your baby startles and cries when undressed or placed on a changing pad or cold bed sheet, and shudders or turns bluish.	Your baby will probably soon adapt to temperature changes. In the meantime, keep towels warming on top of the radiator to cover the changing table, or use a lambskin. Wipe the baby with warm, damp washcloths under a receiving blanket. Postpone immersion baths. Warm up the bed with a hot-water bottle or a heating pad (check for comfort before laying the baby down), or use flannel sheets. Keep booties on day and night, and keep the room comfortably warm.
Bowel movement or urination	The baby squirms, fusses, grunts, and bears down. He may want to nurse, but soon stops. He may start to cry in the middle of a feeding as his colon naturally contracts. The baby should soon produce a bowel movement. If he continues to act this way intermittently without soiling a diaper, he is probably constipated. This is *not* normal behavior during urination.	Straining at urination or frequent constipation should be brought to your doctor's attention. Occasionally a newborn has a constricted anus (see page 101). Your doctor may recommend using a small glycerin suppository to ease uncomfortable bowel movements.

Continued on next page

QUICK REFERENCE GUIDE TO BABIES' CRYING—*Continued*

TYPE OF CRY	DESCRIPTION	WHAT TO DO
Too hot	The baby is irritable and whiny. He may be flushed, sweaty, and breathing rapidly. (Check for fever if the baby seems sick or has had a vaccination in the past day.) You may see red dots—prickly heat—on the baby's face, neck, or shoulders.	Make sure your baby's skin is warm to the touch, but not hot, under his coverings. Overdressing a baby, especially when he has a fever, can cause heatstroke and possibly death. Don't dress the baby for bed in heavy sleepers. Use light blankets.
Boredom or desire for attention	Coos and gurgles build up into protests and wails. As the baby gets older, he may even use a "fake" cry as a bid for attention. Picking up brings an instant halt to the crying.	Carry your baby on your body in a baby pack or sling, or keep him near enough to see you. When no one can hold the baby, looking at a light or through a window may keep a newborn entertained. A mobile or toys may work for a little while with a baby over two months.

start to discover that your baby has hidden likes and dislikes—for example, more or less handling and certain positions may work best for him. Your baby may fall asleep best sitting upright, looking at a table lamp. He may like being swaddled and laid on his right side when put to bed at night, or he might prefer not to have anything bind him, even booties. He may love being in a baby pack, feeling the rhythm of your walking, or, then again, he may hate being constricted that way. Hopefully, you'll discover peak times in the day when he tends to be both alert and content. At these times, you'll want to drop everything in favor of gentle parent-baby play.

All Babies Cry Sometimes

Some babies cry a lot more than others, even though they may be perfectly healthy and their parents very experienced in handling infants. The amount of time your baby spends crying each day may be less than it seems. Though you may feel that your baby is crying twenty-four hours a day, if you carefully record his actual crying times you may discover that his crying isn't really nonstop. Understandably, your feelings of frustration and helplessness may make it seem that your baby cries endlessly.

So how much crying is normal? Opinions vary. Many studies have found that crying episodes start in earnest around three weeks of age, peak at around six weeks, and decrease significantly between three and four months of age. Crying tends to be worst around meal-times—7:00 A.M., 12:00 P.M., and between 5:00 and 6:00 P.M.—with the most crying around dinnertime.[11] Some researchers say babies average an hour and a quarter of crying per day; others say two to four hours' crying per day is normal.

What is normal to these researchers might be quite worrisome to you, and might be considered a cause for alarm in a country where babies are generally given closer nurturing than they are in the United States. In India and Africa babies are carried by their mothers or other family members all day long and kept beside them at night, but here many babies are expected to be content in nonhuman baby holders such as cribs, playpens, car seats, and strollers. And this treatment usually leads to more crying.

Special Babies, Intolerable Cries

When a baby's loud, shrill cries exceed his parents' inherent level of sound tolerance, they may lose their ability to cope. Conditions in pregnancy, such as mild malnutrition of the fetus or toxemia in the mother, can give a baby a high-pitched cry of seven hundred to eight hundred cycles per second instead of the normal three hundred to four hundred cycles per second. Especially high, shrill, or arrhythmical cries can trigger hostile impulses in some parents. Babies who are premature, small for their gestational age, or retarded often have more irritating cries than normal babies, and are also more frequently abused.

Besides sounding terrible, premature babies may look more like little monkeys than like older human babies. When parents of premature babies were asked to rate the effects of watching and hearing a premature baby cry on video, the parents found the experience as upsetting as being repeatedly insulted and being given electric shock.

If your baby's cries make you feel that way, you need extra support. You may be relieved just to know that others share your perception that your baby looks and sounds terrible. With help, you can learn to accept that your baby is not perfect and that he makes special demands on you. Once you recognize that he has special needs, you can work to find ways to help him, rather than letting anger and depression sap your energy. (For help in coping, see chapter 10,

"Taking Care of Yourself," and chapter 11, "Overcoming Stress and Depression.")

When Silence Is a Danger Sign

Just as it's hard to know how much crying is normal for a baby, it's also hard to set standards about how much *silence* is normal. Babies who seldom cry and never protest—even when there is good reason to protest—may be signaling that something is emotionally or physically wrong.

Silent resignation can be even more serious a signal than the loud wails of a protesting baby. A baby who is very passive or sleepy may actually be too "good" for his own survival, for only by protesting can he get the attention he needs to thrive. When a mother brags that her baby sleeps through the night at three weeks of age, the baby's doctor may become concerned, especially if the baby is not gaining weight as expected. The baby is too young to be able to go for such a long period of time without nursing.

As he gets older, a silent baby is much more likely to develop serious psychological disorders than a baby who cries a lot. Of a hundred children between the ages of four and seventeen who were referred to a British psychiatric unit because of severe emotional problems, half were described by their mothers as non-crying babies. Most of the mothers said their babies had been "contented," but psychiatrists described the babies' passivity as "false independence"—a disengagement from human interaction that was the first step in the development of severe emotional disorders.[12]

It's normal for a baby to protest lustily when he is being separated from his parents, particularly during the sensitive attachment phase between seven and twelve months. When babies this age don't protest separation from their parents—when they stop complaining and withdraw during hospital stays, for instance—then nurses and caregivers ought to be alarmed. The baby's mute silence in the face of a strange and threatening environment may signal that he is undergoing deep psychological distress.[13]

Crying, then, can be a sign that a baby is strong and healthy and expects prompt responses from his mother and father. By refusing to be passive, a crying baby makes sure his basic need for nurturance is met.

CHAPTER TWO

The Best Ways to Deal with Crying

WILL YOU SPOIL YOUR BABY by carrying her too much, by answering her cries too quickly, or by getting into the habit of going to her when she wakes up over and over during the night? A lot of parents worry about this—especially when their babies are extra demanding. Fatigue can make you question whether you're falling into a trap of being manipulated by your baby. Doctors and relatives may try to convince you that you are.

"Maybe I'm being too soft on her. Maybe my baby needs to be shown who's boss," you say to yourself. So you stop going to your baby when she cries, or you chide her for making demands. But she only cries harder and longer.

Research has shown that parents who are the most afraid of spoiling their babies are the most likely to produce children who act spoiled. By taking longer to answer, these parents get accustomed to the crying, and so distance themselves from their babies even more. The baby's trust in her caregivers begins to erode, which makes her quicker to cry and harder to soothe. Eventually she grows into a clingy, overly demanding, and insecure toddler.[14]

Parents' attitudes even during pregnancy can affect how they respond to their babies after birth. One study showed that expectant parents who said they were hesitant to pick up babies for fear of spoiling them were more liable to produce babies who cried long and frequently than were expectant parents who believed babies' cries should be answered right away.[15]

Studies have also shown that the longer a parent takes to answer a baby's cries, the longer it takes to soothe the baby. The critical cutoff

"My mother and my mother-in-law keep telling me I'm catering to my baby. They say that if I pick her up every time she cries, she will always cry, and that I will become a slave to her. They think she has to learn early that crying doesn't pay. It breaks my heart to hear my baby crying for me, and to try to pretend I don't hear her."

point for answering a baby's cries is *a minute and a half*. If a parent takes longer than a minute and a half to answer, the amount of time required to quiet the baby increases by three, four, or in some cases fifty times.[16]

The work of Dr. Mary B. Ainsworth and Dr. Sylvia Bell at Johns Hopkins University confirms the importance of quick responses. Babies who were answered quickly during the first few months after birth cried less often and for shorter periods of time in later months. When parents didn't respond as rapidly, their babies were more liable to be fussier. The quickly answered babies seemed to be able to invest their energies in finding other, more pleasant ways of communicating. Instead of becoming clingy toddlers, they were more likely to demonstrate healthy independence at the appropriate stage of maturity.[17]

Babies Are Human Beings, a book published in 1954, sums up what has now been confirmed by research:

> Most spoiled children are those who as babies never had essential gratification owing to a mistaken attempt to fit them into a rigid regimen. The spoiled child who has missed satisfaction as a baby adopts the efficient technique of whining and temper tantrums to get what he wants. The mechanism of spoiling is the neglect of needs rather than overindulgence. . . . Responsive adults breed responsive babies, and . . . rigid disciplinarians of babies at this age breed spoiled, unhappy children with no confidence in themselves or their parents.[18]

The Parent-Baby Dance

A tall, sturdily built woman, Ellen Grayson is the mother of eight thriving children, one of whom just left for college. She breastfed and cared for all eight at home while they were young. I figured that if anyone knew how to soothe a crying baby, she did.

One day I watched her very closely as she scooped up a red-faced, screaming three-week-old from his distraught mother and put her expert baby-soothing techniques into action. She planted tiny Josh against her shoulder, holding him firmly by the buttocks with one hand and gently cupping his head with the other.

Then she began to dance. She took eight or ten rhythmical paces forward, turned around, and took eight or ten paces to where she had started: step, pause . . . step, pause. Her hand gently moved down to

Josh's back, patting with each pause. His toes uncurled.

She continued her walk, adding sounds that I had never heard used with a baby before. She produced deep guttural groans—the kind of groans that people make when they're having an orgasm. The groans welled forth each time she came to a pause in her rhythmical stepping.

Groan-pat-pause-walk, groan-pat-pause-walk, the dance went on. Josh's hands uncurled, and then he let out a huge, chin-quivering sigh that racked his tiny body. Ellen continued to firmly hold him in place, not even stopping to check his expression. He heaved another deep sigh, as if to say "Home, at last!," and his eyes fluttered to half-mast. Within ten minutes of Ellen's beginning her mothering performance, Josh fell into a deep sleep, his body limp.

I found out later that Ellen had learned the dance from her mother, who had learned it from *her* mother; the skill had been passed down from generation to generation. Essential to the success of such a dance is the ability to tune in to the baby while tuning out the rest of the world. Ellen was able to break down the physical barriers between herself and Josh and to speak a primitive body language to him. She communicated her own calm while at the same time absorbing his tension. Her dance told the baby, "I am completely here for you. Forget about the noises and glare of the world. You are safe." By the end of the dance, not only was the baby freed into profound rest, but Ellen was transported into a gentle, satisfied state as well.

Were I to analyze what went on between Ellen and Josh, I could isolate certain potent soothing techniques that are known to affect babies. They include physical closeness, rhythmical motion, and repetitive deep sound, which in this case vibrated both Ellen's chest and the baby. But the other element—the tender effacing of boundaries into a mutual state of peaceful surety—is subjective, but very, very real. Once you've begun to experience it with your baby, you'll remember how it feels long after your baby grows up.

Staying Close

Human babies are made to be carried. They come equipped with reflexes and abilities designed to ensure their physical attachment to parents. Newborns can wiggle like snakes to get to their mothers' breasts for nursing. Their tiny clutching fingers and toes and their startle response (or Moro reflex), which ends with fingers closing in tight fists, all help to keep them attached to their parents' bodies.

"In most cultures, a baby is attached to the mother's body in some way until it can sit up by itself for long periods, and often for the first year of life. It is as if the baby is still part of the mother, though now outside her body, rather like a kangaroo in its mother's pouch. The baby is fed whenever he nuzzles up to the breast."

SHEILA KITZINGER
The Crying Baby[21]

Bearded or hairy-chested fathers, and mothers with long hair or necklaces, can attest to the strength of a baby's grasp.

Likewise, nature gives mothers a strong internal drive to keep their babies close. Perhaps you've experienced the phenomenon of "chest hunger"—a powerful urge to pull your baby in toward you. Once your baby is enfolded against your body, the feeling disappears. Mothers separated from their babies by hospitalization or permanent loss sometimes find their hunger for closeness turns into almost unbearable physical pain.

The composition of breast milk discourages long separations between mother and baby. Mammals who must leave their offspring behind while they search for food produce milk high in protein and fat, made to sustain infrequent feedings, every two to fifteen hours. But human beings, like other mammals that carry their offspring around with them, produce milk low in protein and fat, and high in sugar. This milk is made for feeding almost continually, every hour and a half (or less) to four hours.[19]

In all human societies other than that of the industrialized West, babies are in physical contact with other people almost continuously. At night, they sleep beside their mothers and siblings. During the day, baby-carrying responsibilities may be shared among mother, grandmother, and siblings as young as six years. Whereas American babies are held only 16 to 23 percent of the time, African !Kung babies, for example, spend as much as 90 percent of their time directly on their mothers' bodies. In such a society, a baby's cries are taken seriously and answered quickly. Long bouts of crying are rare.

Babies who are carried all day continuously experience a world rich in sensory stimulation, but many babies in our society are isolated in an emotional and sensory vacuum. They are expected to cry long and hard to get what they need, to sleep alone in cribs in their own rooms, and to spend their days sitting placidly in lifeless holding devices such as chairs, walkers, and playpens. Sadly, over seventy thousand babies are rushed to U.S. emergency rooms every year because of injuries related to such baby products. Many times, the babies are injured trying to get to their parents.[20]

In a sense, your baby undergoes a second, out-of-the-womb, gestation against your body after birth. She is at your mercy to provide her with the milk and warmth she needs to survive. No wonder she cries when you lay her down before she is asleep, or wakes after only a few minutes of sleeping alone!

Giving in to nature, if you have been fighting it, may bring both you and your baby great relief. With the baby held securely against you in a sling or baby pack, you can go about your work without continual interruptions. If you keep your baby close to you both night and day, you will know when she begins to root or whimper, and she will rarely need to wait for your attention. When you no longer must spend long periods soothing a scared and angry baby, you may find yourself calmer and happier.

Your Baby's Shutdown System

Although your baby can't walk away from situations that are stressful, she *can* shut the world out. She is protected from excess stimulation by the immaturity of her nervous system. Because her nerve pathways can handle only a few incoming signals at a time in the first months, she can't, for example, pay attention to the noise of a rattle and suck at the same time. Certain incoming signals, particularly those that employ her most mature systems—her sense of hearing, her sense of balance, and her sucking reflexes, take priority over others. When strong signals come through these systems, competing signals are screened out or muted.

If your baby is extremely stressed, she may enter a state that appears to be sleep, but is really total shutdown. After circumcision without anesthesia, for example, a newborn will usually shut down into what appears to be a deep sleep, rather than fussing and crying as an older baby might. During the shutdown period the baby will be hard to awaken, but once awake he'll be irritable and hard to soothe. This may go on for several days.

"Gaze aversion" is another way babies shut out the world. Your baby may refuse to look at you. First she may narrow her eyes and look to the side, and then she may turn her head away. She is letting you know that you're getting too intrusive, and that she needs a break. Parents who don't understand this signal may keep trying to catch the baby's eye, talking even more insistently to her or poking her to try to get her to play with them.

The best way of responding to your baby's gaze aversion is by imitating her. When your baby starts to turn away, turn away yourself. Your baby may give you a furtive glance and then try to engage your attention again, as though she feels reassured by the fact you got her message.

"Sometimes my baby won't even look at me. If I get closer he turns his head completely away. If I step back from him, I can see him starting to peek at me. He just wants space. If I keep talking and move back a little more, he'll usually glance at me again."

"We couldn't let her cry. We would walk her for hours or rock her. Our baby sling would help. As soon as we tried to lay her down, she would cry. She needed walking. She just wanted to be close."

"Our colicky baby liked being rocked in a rocking chair with a not-too-hot water bottle against his belly, dancing with us to music, going outside for a walk or a ride in the stroller while we talked to him about things we saw, and swinging in an automatic baby swing."

Finding Good Soothing Strategies

Each baby has her own preferred ways of being calmed. The power of a particular calming technique for an individual baby depends on her inborn sensitivities. Visually oriented babies may be soothed by looking out the window or at a light. Those with acute auditory awareness may respond to certain kinds of music (some preferring Mozart and others new age or country-western). Babies most sensitive to touch may respond well to being held or enclosed, and babies who love action—those who are constantly in motion, their arms and legs circling—may respond best to being moved around, rocked, and jiggled.

As a parent, you probably have your own preferences among soothing methods. You may have learned some of your techniques from watching other parents, but on the whole you probably respond much as your own parents did when you were a baby and child. Some parents are verbal—talking, humming, and singing lullabies—whereas others are more physical—rocking, jiggling, and walking with the baby.

A study of how mothers comforted their babies found many variations:

> Some mothers gently rocked the [crying] infant from side to side, others patted his back or rubbed the nape of his neck. Some rocked and patted at the same time. Some massaged the baby. Others jostled the infant, moving him up and down at a fast pace as they held him in their arms. Some mothers accompanied their movement by humming or speaking softly in a soothing voice. Others remained silent. No matter what form the action, the infants were soon quieted. They seemed to respond to their mother's particular technique, to fit to it, and to be calmed by it.[22]

Together, you and your baby will find techniques that marry her preferences and yours. The "Basic Shutdown Techniques" chart may give you some ideas.

THE JOY OF MOTION. Motion helps to teach your baby about the relationship between her body and the world around her. Some scientists believe that immobilizing a baby for a long time can cause certain nerve pathways in the baby's brain to degenerate, just as arm muscles shrink when you break a bone and have it in a cast for a long time.

Motion messages are transmitted to your baby's brain by the vestibular system deep within her ear, behind the drum. Small,

BASIC SHUTDOWN TECHNIQUES

ACTION	DESCRIPTION	HELPFUL TECHNIQUES AND DEVICES
Sucking	By focusing on his sucking, your baby can completely tune out external signals. He may learn to calm himself by sucking his wrist, fingers, or fist. If you nurse him while he gets an injection, he is less likely to cry long and hard.	Keep your newborn's hands exposed so he can suck on them. Besides the breast, a pacifier or your little finger, soft pad up, can be used in the early months to help your baby remain calm. (Never use a stuffed bottle nipple as a pacifier—the baby would swallow too much air.)
Sounds	A baby's hearing (unlike his vision) is quite well developed even before birth. Certain sounds block out other stimuli, from inside or outside her body, so she can relax and fall asleep. The most effective sounds are monotonous and droning, or rhythmical and repetitive.	Talk to your baby quietly but continuously, sing softly, or play calming recorded music. *Other sound sources:* vacuum cleaner, dishwasher, clothes dryer, white noise from a radio station off the air, commercial recordings of womb noises. *(Note: Sensitivity is in order. Some sounds may comfort and lull your baby, while others may frighten her. You don't want to shock her into shutdown!)*
Motion	Motion acts as a powerful inhibitor of minor discomforts, and rhythmical motion stimulates your baby's vestibular system.	*Actions:* Walk with the baby on your shoulder, against your chest, or on your back. Swing her up and down or side to side in wide arcs. Lay her face-down on your lap and move your knees up and down. If all else fails, take her for a ride in the car. *Devices:* Sling or baby pack, rocking chair, cradle, carriage, baby swing (some have cradle attachments). *(Note: To be most effective, rocking must be fast and vigorous.)*
Visual stimulation	Some babies calm down when they see something that fascinates them.	*Favorite things for a baby to watch:* the light and shadows in a tree's foliage, the glow from a lamp, a mobile, complex wallpaper patterns. *Best positions:* against your shoulder, semi-upright in a baby seat, lying on his back, or propped on his side.

Continued on next page

BASIC SHUTDOWN TECHNIQUES—*Continued*

ACTION	DESCRIPTION	HELPFUL TECHNIQUES AND DEVICES
Immobilization and swaddling	Restraining a baby can sometimes help to inhibit an overactive startle response. Sometimes just holding down an arm or a leg can help prevent a crying jag.	*Swaddle the baby:* Lay her on a receiving blanket with one corner positioned over her head, one below her feet, and one beyond each arm. Fold the bottom corner over the feet. Pull in the side corners and wrap them around the baby's body so her arms are held still. (A diaper pin will keep the blanket fastened in a cocoon.)
Wedging	Babies appear instinctively to seek out boundaries—particularly around their backs and heads. A newborn placed in a crib will naturally move to a corner because he longs for the comfort and security of close confinement.	Let the baby sleep curled at your side, with her head in your armpit, your arm at her back. Or put the baby, wrapped in a blanket, on her right side in a crib, her back against the crib's bumpers and her head touching the top padded corner. Place a firm stuffed toy or small pillow against her abdomen to brace her in this position. *(Note: To avoid any risk of suffocation, don't place pillows near the baby's face.)* You can also put the baby to bed in a drawer removed from a chest or in an open small padded box. *(Be sure the padding fits without ridges or gaps that could allow suffocation.)*

chalky particles tickle tiny hairs that float in two jelly-filled chambers (the *sacculus* and *utriculus*). Each time a baby moves her head, nearby nerves transmit the tickling message to her brain, telling her her position in relation to gravity. Curving tubes filled with liquid (the *semicircular canals*) give out signals telling the baby's brain when she is rocking, spinning, moving up and down, or making other motions. Getting dizzy from spinning around and getting sick from a rough plane ride are effects of this apparatus.

Your baby is born accustomed to a great deal of motion: she has been rocking with your every movement for the past nine months. (And whenever you sat still for long in pregnancy she probably started in kicking, as if to say, "Get moving, Mom!") Throughout infancy, most children continue to love—and demand—a lot of motion. They are soothed by being walked, rocked in a rocking chair or a cradle, swung in a swing or hammock, or jiggled in a baby carriage with springs. Your baby will probably love dancing to music with you.

When you are trying to soothe a fussy baby, the speed of your movements is important. You'll want to rock or dance rather vigorously, close to your own walking pace. Whether you move your baby back and forth or from side to side, and whether she is lying down or sitting up, matters less.[23] (Caution: Because a baby's head is large relative to her weak neck, hard shaking can injure her. Support your baby's head when you dance together. Avoid jerking, repeatedly tossing, or whirling the baby, and don't jog while carrying her on your back or shoulders with her head unsupported.)

Manufacturers have come up with a variety of products to provide motion for babies, such as wind-up swings and devices that fasten onto a crib to make it jiggle. Most such products, however, are only substitutes for the motion and comfort of another human body.

An exception are baby packs and slings. These allow parents to hold their babies on the front, back, or hip as they go about their business, hands free. Many designs are available, quite a few of them from mother-owned, home-based businesses (see the ads in *Mothering* and *Compleat Mother* magazines). In many countries an unsewn strip of cloth serves the same purpose. A study found that babies who were carried 50 percent more than others cried 43 percent less overall and 51 percent less during the evening hours (4:00 P.M. to 12:00 A.M.).[24]

When you can't hold the baby or just need a break (especially at dinnertime), automatic rocking cradles and wind-up swings can be helpful. Experienced parents suggest choosing the swing model that offers the longest running time, since the baby may be jarred awake when you try to recrank the device. (More expensive, battery-operated models are available, but they don't offer the same reassuring, rhythmical clacking sound.) For a newborn, you may want to buy an adaptable model that comes with both a bassinet and a swing seat, since young babies are unable to sit up well and may not like the front-to-back motion as much as the side-to-side. If you do put a small baby in a swing seat, she should be secured by a sash or a small belt so she doesn't fall forward into the padded front bar of the swing, unable to sit herself back up.

One invention of questionable benefit is the SleepTight, which attaches to the springs of a crib to make it vibrate, and also makes a noise intended to sound like wind whooshing past the closed windows of a car. The device sometimes appears to soothe babies, but

"My baby required motion and constant carrying during his first six months to keep from crying. I finally discovered that a hammock strung up on one side of the kitchen was a great help. I could rock and rest and my hands were freed if I wanted to read or knit."

"Mothers probably have soothed their babies by humming or singing to them since time immemorial. Many, if not all, adults have a non-verbal vocabulary of cooing and clucking nonsense sounds that they trot out, consciously or unconsciously, only for communication with the very young."

DR. RITA B. EISENBERG[26]

looks may be deceiving. Some researchers believe a baby may shut down her system in defense against the stress the contraption causes. (Constant jiggling, besides, may stress a crib's hardware to the breaking point, so if you install a SleepTight be sure to monitor the structural integrity of your baby's crib.)

A few babies don't like motion at all; they become unglued if they are jarred. Often born prematurely, these babies have an overactive Moro reflex, which causes them to startle at every motion. They may ask for almost complete stillness in the first few months after birth. They need to be carried in slow motion, and some may even feel better being held in a pillow at first, rather than being directly touched. Some prefer firm massage to light finger touches.

THE POWER OF CONVERSATION AND MUSIC. "Why should I talk to Leslie when she can't even understand me?" Nancy Whitter asked me as she sat watching television while her four-week-old baby, Leslie, fussed for attention in her infant seat. What Nancy, like many first-time mothers, did not realize is that babies are very sensitive to the human voice and language.

People once thought that babies came into the world as senseless creatures, deaf and nearly blind. The baby's brain was considered "a blank slate" onto which life's lessons would be written. Now researchers are discovering that babies, even hours after birth, have amazing abilities linked to language.

Hearing is one of the earliest neurological systems to mature in the developing fetus. Babies can hear voices, music, and other sounds long before they are born, and there is little doubt that after birth they are excited by sounds that were familiar to them in the womb. One mother of a fussy baby, for example, played the cello all during her pregnancy, practicing one difficult passage over and over. After the baby was born she stopped playing for a few weeks. When she again picked up the cello and began to play the difficult passage, the baby's eyes widened, and he abruptly became silent and still, listening with fascination to the familiar melody. He was hearing an old favorite!

Although your newborn's vision isn't nearly as well developed as her hearing, she'll enjoy watching your face as you talk to her. Babies love to watch faces: when infants only minutes old were presented a choice of pictures—a blank square, a scrambled human face, or a proper human face—they turned their bodies 180 degrees to keep their focus on the drawing of the proper face.[25] Until they are about two months old, babies can focus clearly upon a face only when it is about 8 inches away from their eyes—but this is exactly the distance most people instinctively choose for conversing with their babies.

Babies prefer the human voice to other sounds. Given a choice among rattles, babies choose those with frequencies closest to that of a human voice.[27]

Slow-motion films demonstrate that very soon after birth babies move their bodies in synchrony to the sounds of human language. They don't do the same "dance" when presented with nonsense syllables. And babies *expect* us to have social exchanges with them. When parents are told to be silent and stone-faced in front of their babies, the babies quickly show signs of surprise followed by anger and frustration.[28]

Every baby likes her own mother's voice the most. Dr. Anthony DeCasper invented a device that allowed babies to select among recorded voices by changing the speed at which they sucked on a pacifier. Babies only one and a half to three days old sucked at the exact rate that allowed them to listen to their own mothers' voices.[29]

All babies, and especially fussy, unhappy ones, need a steady diet of human vocal sounds. You might give your baby a running commentary about what you are doing. Converse with her as you soothe her. To engage her attention, slow down your speech, hold her about 8 inches from your face, and slowly nod your head as you speak. When you sing or make guttural sounds for your baby, lay her on your shoulder or chest so she can feel your vibrations.

Most babies respond positively to music, especially their parents' singing. It's nice to learn some lullabies or to try old church hymns, but anything will do. Making up your own lyrics may help you to relax. Some mothers of fussy babies suggest making up mildly threatening lyrics—about how you'll sail off on a ship if the baby doesn't stop crying, for instance—as a humorous way of relieving your frustration.

Just like adults, babies have different musical preferences. Try out different kinds of music when your baby is alert and calm. If she likes the music, she will probably become still, or make sounds or motions that show you she is enjoying herself. Hopefully, the music that your baby prefers matches your own taste!

Music can be therapeutic for you, too. You may want to get a small cassette player with earphones to wear around the house. The sound reproduction of these tiny players is often as good as that of costly stereos. The earphones won't close out your baby's cries, but will mute them a bit. The best sounds are those that arouse intense feelings of pleasure, to counter the feelings of frustration or annoy-

What'll we do with the baby-o?
What'll we do with the baby-o?
We'll wrap it up in calico,
Send it to its daddy-o.

AMERICAN FOLK SONG

"My baby didn't want to be held when he was trying to go to sleep. If I just put him down, he would fret for a few minutes and then fall quickly off to sleep. If I held him, he would get more and more restless and unhappy until he was crying. He seemed to want to sleep on his own."

ance aroused by your baby's screams. Since no one can hear the music but you, this is often the perfect answer at 4:00 in the morning.

THE MAGIC OF TOUCH. Patting and massaging are both old-fashioned soothing techniques that work for babies who are not too "skin-sensitive"—that is, who do not get upset by being uncovered and touched. Back rubs can help a baby who is already relaxed to get to sleep. And if your baby is fussy, patting her on her back in a steady rhythm can help to calm her.

Massaging your baby can help to foster closeness between the two of you. In the beginning, make sure the baby is relaxed and happy; later you may be able to use massage for soothing. A good time to start may be just after your baby has had a nice warm bath (or even during the bath). Make sure the room is warm, and rub your hands together to warm them. You may want to leave a young baby partly covered. Oil isn't necessary, but if you like it, choose a cold-pressed vegetable oil. Allow it to warm in your hand before applying it to the baby's skin. Begin stroking with the lightest touch; increase the pressure if your baby seems to like it.

If your baby has abdominal pain, massaging her belly can help move gas bubbles along. Lay the baby on her back. Grasp her by the ankles with one hand, and gently bend her knees so her belly stays relaxed. Now begin the "I Love You" massage, as Dr. William Sears describes it in his book *The Fussy Baby.* Picture a large upside down *U* on your baby's belly. This represents your baby's large intestine, or colon, along which gas passes. It begins on your baby's lower right (your left), crosses below her rib cage, and runs down her left side (your right) to end at her lower left at the rectum. Make a single, gentle stroke (the *I*) from your baby's rib cage down to the hip on her left side (your right side). This will move gas down toward her rectum. Then stroke from your baby's right side to her left, just below the ribs, and down the left side again (making an upside-down *L*). Finally, begin at the baby's lower right side, near the leg, and stroke upward, across the middle again, and back down the left side (making an upside-down *U*).[30]

Some parents report that their fussy babies have been helped by chiropractors. Certain adjustments, such as for a misaligned vertebra, appear to bring about relief to some babies.[31] It's worth asking other parents for the name of a good chiropractor in your community who works with babies and children. I would strongly suggest foregoing any X-rays, however, because of possible harm from cumulative X-ray exposure.

Letting Off Steam

After the first few months, some babies are able to simply turn off and fall asleep when they get tired, but others get more and more wound up and fussy as they become fatigued. They may need to cry a few minutes before falling off to sleep.

Even the most closely nurtured babies have times when they need to let off steam. For example, Mayan Indian babies in southern Mexico are allowed to nurse whenever they want to, and sometimes mothers keep their breasts in the babies' mouths like pacifiers. Although it is rare to hear a baby cry during the day, Mayan babies sometimes cry for several hours at night. No one worries about it, though; as the Maya say, "When everyone gets quiet, it's the baby's turn to do the talking."[32]

You can tell if your baby needs a few minutes of crying before sleep by listening to how she cries. Do her cries start off loud, become quieter and quieter, then stop and start again, until she falls off to sleep? Or do her cries build to higher and higher peaks, until she is wide-awake and frantic? If the latter is the case, you have mis-read your baby. She needs you!

Sometimes your baby may awaken and cry momentarily before falling back to sleep again. You needn't turn on the light, pick her up, or nurse her immediately. If she is hungry or needs you, her cries will become more insistent. But if she is just going through a brief restless spell, her cries will soften and then stop.

"If you run right over to the baby's crib and ask, 'Sweetie, what is the trouble? Are you hungry? Are you wet?' your baby is going to hear your voice and wake up for your attention.... Listen before you barge in.... Some babies fuss and thrash around for a while and then settle down for more sleep."

MAMA RUBY WRIGHT
Old-Fashioned Baby Care[33]

*"There were days
when I cried when
my friends talked
about their babies
taking three-hour
naps!"*

CHAPTER THREE

*Why Your Baby Doesn't
"Sleep Like a Baby"*

NOSY AUNT CLARA LEANS DOWN to take a peek at your baby snoozing in his stroller. She asks the question that people always ask new parents: "Is he a *good* baby?" This is followed by "Does he sleep through the night?"

By now you've learned to hedge a bit. "I think *all* babies are good, don't you, Aunt Clara? *Why* do you ask?"

Soon you discover that Aunt Clara, your own parents, your boss, and your pediatrician—all have unrealistic assumptions about how your baby should act. He is expected to lead a perfectly regulated life suited to the convenience of you and everyone else. He's supposed to act always like the gurgling cherubs in TV ads for diapers and baby toys. He's expected to be the satisfied crib potato—amenable, never protesting, and eager to get a solid eight or more hours of beauty rest every night. If he doesn't live up to the perfect baby myth, then he's a failure long before he even reaches first grade.

When parents brag about their little darling "sleeping through the night," they usually mean that he's sleeping without interruption for one long stretch each night—say, between midnight and 5:00 A.M. Rarely will babies sleep through the night from birth. When they do, doctors worry about them. They may not be taking in all the milk they need to grow normally.

Typically a newborn sleeps one and a half to three hours at a stretch, with some doubling up of sleep periods here and there. The development of regular night sleeping patterns is gradual and usually starts to emerge around the third month.

There are as many variations in babies' sleep patterns as there are babies. Some newborns sleep as much as twenty-three out of twenty-four hours, especially if they have got a dose of their mothers' drugs during labor. These little ones, placid at first, may turn irritable and sleepless a few weeks later. Other babies may appear to need only ten or twelve hours of sleep in twenty-four hours. Still others start to sleep through the night after the second or third week only to begin night waking all over again several months later or during toddlerhood.

Although most babies gradually decrease the number of night feedings, some make an abrupt transition—one night it seems they forget to wake up, then they never awaken at night again. Others sleep increasingly longer in the mornings while still waking often in

---

FACTS ABOUT BABY SLEEP

✔ A baby's sleep-wake patterns begin to form even before birth.

✔ The typical pattern for newborns is to sleep during the day and be awake at night—the very opposite of their parents' cycles.

✔ Most newborns sleep one and a half to three hours at a stretch.

✔ The rare baby may "sleep through the night"—for a stretch of five hours or more—as early as ten days after birth, but the average age for doing so is three months.

✔ Erratic sleep cycles in newborns have been associated with prolonged labors, lack of oxygen, and other birth complications.

✔ A baby may be safer sleeping on his back or side than on his belly. Evidence from several countries suggests a possible link between the face-down position and Sudden Infant Death Syndrome.

✔ Feeding a baby solid foods won't make him sleep longer, and if he is allergic to substances in the food, it may make him awaken even more frequently.

✔ Between one-third and one quarter of all children continue to wake up during the night even after one year of age.

"No matter how carefully I planned my day with the baby, it seemed that nearly every time my husband and I sat down for dinner, the baby would start to cry. It was impossible to eat while she was crying, and by the time she'd been diapered or burped or just comforted, my husband had finished eating, and my dinner was cold. Since dinner was the time I'd counted on for the two of us to relax together, I soon began to feel very frustrated and angry at myself for not managing better."

GERALDINE YOUCHS
"First Baby in the House"[34]

the night. And still others are completely erratic in their night waking, with no predictability for months on end.

In one study, 70 percent of the babies slept from around midnight to between 5:00 and 6:00 A.M. by the age of three months. By six months of age, 83 percent had "settled." But don't count on your baby keeping to this schedule. Approximately *half* the babies studied started night waking again in the months to follow. And one out of every ten never slept through the night during the first year.[35] In fact, one-fourth of all two-year-olds wake their parents up two or more nights a week.

The Science of Baby Sleep

In the early 1900s doctors claimed that the reason infants sleep so much was because of a lack of oxygen to the brain from drinking too much mother's milk. Later on it was believed that the baby's immature brain got fatigued much faster than an adult's and thus needed more rest. Scientists are now peering into the crib with a number of precise instruments to find out what babies' sleep is really like. They've discovered that the old phrase "he sleeps like a baby" couldn't be more wrong in its assumption about how babies sleep.

Because a baby's brain, like an adult's, operates with detectable low levels of electricity, scientists use a measuring device called an electroencephalogram, or EEG, to identify sleep patterns. By taping electrodes onto a baby's head, they can record the electrical activity of his brain. The recording takes the form of jagged lines made by an oscillating pen on a moving sheet of paper. The lines represent brain waves.

Brain-wave measurements show that the rest-activity cycles of babies in the last months before birth correspond to their mothers'. But it's not the baby who comes to sleep like his mother; it's the mother, rather, who because of profound hormonal changes alters her sleeping patterns to match her baby's. Immediately after giving birth, the mother returns to her normal sleep patterns, but the newborn's sleep cycle maintains the rest-activity patterns established before birth.[36]

Brain-wave patterns show that newborns undergo three very distinct phases of sleep: active sleep, quiet sleep, and a transitional phase sometimes called the basic rest-activity cycle, or BRAC. A baby falls first into active sleep, then has a period of BRAC, then quiet sleep, then active sleep again. This cycle is repeated throughout the night.

Another state directly related to sleep is drowsiness. When your baby is getting ready to go to sleep, his eyelids turn red and seem to get very heavy. He may rub his eyes. They may flutter open and closed, and they have a glazed appearance, as though they are unfocused. Within one to two minutes he will fall into active sleep.

The term *active sleep* is well chosen, for when the amount of physical restlessness that a baby displays during this phase is measured by motion-sensitive mattresses, it is found that a baby is often more active during active sleep than he is during normal wakefulness! You can see his eyes moving under closed or partially opened eyelids that may flutter every so often. He may move his mouth—smiling, grimacing, chewing, chomping, or sucking. And he may cry briefly before going right back to sleep again.

When your baby awakens in the night, he's coming out of an active sleep phase. He makes about nine transitions in the night between active and quiet sleep, and it is in these shifts that he is most likely to cry out, root for the breast, lift up his head to look around, turn himself over, or wake up fully. About an hour after falling asleep, and about every hour thereafter through the night, many babies predictably cry out briefly as they move into another active sleep episode.

When your baby has moved into *quiet sleep*, he is very still. His breathing is regular. You can lift up his hand and it falls back down without waking him. His eyelids are firmly closed and his face seems totally relaxed. He makes few or no mouth movements. If you happen to jar the bed during a period of quiet sleep, he may startle but keep right on sleeping.[37]

A simple test to see if your baby is in quiet sleep or active sleep is to gently open one eyelid. If he's in quiet sleep, his eyes are rolled back in his head. But if he's in active sleep, he'll stare straight at you, his body still somewhat tense. (Sometimes new parents mistake a baby in active sleep for an awake one, and try to feed him while he is half-conscious. It doesn't work.)

Whereas adults spend about one-fourth of their sleeping hours in active sleep, full-term newborns spend about half their sleeping time in this phase, and premature babies as much as 80 percent. Babies clearly need more active sleep than grownups, although the reasons for this are not fully understood. Active sleep may be involved in brain growth. During active sleep, oxygen intake increases, blood pressure in the brain rises, and the circulation of blood to the brain increases as much as 50 percent over that of quiet sleep.

Young babies are slow to enter quiet sleep. All parents know the

"Don't make any decisions in the wee hours of the morning, such as weaning, giving the baby away tomorrow, or leaving for Tahiti by yourself. You're not fully awake and aware, and often things will look different in the morning."

game of carefully tiptoeing, inch by inch, to the bed, only to have the phone ring. Too bad! Your baby wakes right up. Drowsiness turns into full-blown crying.

The amount of time required to fall from drowsiness into quiet sleep decreases as the baby matures. Whereas an awake two-month-old takes an average of 27 minutes to get to sleep, a six-month-old takes only about 16 minutes. By about three months of age, a baby begins to fall directly into quiet sleep, skipping the active sleep stage, as adults do. Interestingly, three months is the same age at which fussy babies start to calm down.

Your Baby Doesn't Learn to Sleep

Your baby's sleeping patterns change naturally as his body's systems mature. Newborns aren't equipped with day-night body cycles; they alternate between sleeping and waking throughout the day and night, regardless of what is happening around them. It's not until about the fourth month after birth that the typical baby spends most of the day awake and sleeps longer stretches during the night. By then, the baby's bodily cycles—of high and low temperature, heart rate, and urine excretion, for instance—have become more regulated.[38] The start of sleeping through the night coincides with the appearance of day-night rhythms and the excretion in the baby's body of an important hormone, cortisol, that helps to regulate metabolism.[39]

You can't teach your baby to sleep through the night; it isn't a skill that can be learned. But when the time is right, your baby's inborn master clock will set all of his internal operations in harmonious cycles, and his day and night rhythms will become more predictable.

"Good" and "Bad" Sleepers

Perhaps the hardest thing about caring for an extra-demanding baby is that you rarely get a break. Babies who are irregular, unadaptable, intense, and unhappy sleep about two hours less each night and one hour less during the day than easy babies do.[40] As Dr. William Sears writes, "Parents of a high need child will often describe him as 'exhausting but bright.' These children seem to be constantly awake and aware, by day and by night, as though they possess an internal light bulb that is always on."[41] Although their extraordinary sensitivity has its rewards later, these fussy, wakeful children are very hard on their parents for the first year or two.

Sometimes irregular patterns signal slower-than-normal neurological development in a baby. Unusual brain-wave patterns appear in quiet sleep when a baby isn't developing on a normal timetable. When babies have been severely damaged during birth, both quiet and active sleep phases become totally disorganized. Babies with milder degrees of birth trauma, and those of diabetic or heroin-addicted mothers, have altered patterns of quiet sleep.

There may be a connection between long labors and sleep disruptions in babies after the first few months. Babies of mothers whose labors averaged twelve to thirteen hours are more likely to be night wakers than babies of mothers whose labors averaged only six to nine hours. Night wakers are more likely to have had difficulty establishing breathing after birth, and to have had significantly lower ratings for skin color, muscle tone, and reflex irritability.[42]

Just as with babies' crying, scientists are now recording and studying babies' sleep-wake patterns. Using EEGs, one study precisely defined ninety-four different characteristics of babies' sleep. Such studies may some day help doctors to diagnose brain damage immediately after birth. Doctors may also be able to predict which babies will sleep well and which ones are destined to be night owls.[43]

"If you're up a lot at night, try not to look at the clock. It can be very depressing to know that you've been up three times in one hour, or you've been up for two hours, or you've only got two hours of sleep left until the older children wake up for school."

The Danger of a Baby's Sleeping Alone

Babies depend on their parents both day and night. In industrialized societies such as ours, the stresses of work and rigid time schedules have led parents to seek ways to ensure themselves enough sleep at night, often at the cost of their babies' well-being. From birth, parents pressure babies to sleep for artificially prolonged periods without food or human contact. Isolated babies are less protected from physical harm than babies sleeping with their parents (over one hundred U.S. babies die each year in crib-related accidents). Sleeping alone may also affect a baby's emotional security.

By studying the nightly sleeping rhythms of infant monkeys, researchers are getting a clearer understanding of the way human babies sleep. The sleep patterns of monkeys are very close to those of humans, although human babies are far more physically immature at birth.

"No other society prepares its children for independence as we do. We feel that the first step in building an independent character begins with early nighttime separation from parents. Many children find this a harsh lesson.... Children express their loneliness by crying. They're trying to say, 'I want to be with you. I don't want to be abandoned.' In other societies and in other animal species families sleep in the same room. In our culture, youngsters are put in a room by themselves, the light is turned off, the door is shut, and that's all."

DR. WILSE WEBB
Professor of Psychology
The University of Florida[46]

When infants of some monkey species are forced to endure separation from their mothers during the night, the infants' sleeping patterns show profound alterations, including a marked shortening of quiet sleep episodes. After the separation, a mother's capability for caring for her infant lessens. For a period of time after reunion with her offspring, she is unable to respond to her infant's cues as well as she could before the separation.[44]

The behavior of human infants in hospitals and other institutions shows that human babies, too, are severely distressed by isolation from their parents. At first a baby cries and appears extremely upset; then he moves into a stage of sad-eyed despair. He may make hopeless sounding cries, as if he expects no comforting, and avoid eye-to-eye contact. Finally he may move into apathy and detachment. He no longer protests being picked up by strangers and may lay for hours in motionless withdrawal. These reactions are similar to those shown by severely abused babies.

Even though a baby may appear to have accepted separation in the hospital, he may have lost much of his ability to form emotional ties and to sustain relationships. After he returns home, he may still be detached; he may treat his parents as though they were strangers. In time, he may become overly dependent, demanding, and clingy.

The enforced nightly isolation of babies from their parents that is typical in our society may reinforce long-term sleeplessness in babies. Mini-cycles of protest, despair, apathy, and then detachment may be occurring nightly in American homes. The fear of isolation can cause the baby to stay awake, since deep sleep requires a sense of safety and security from dangers, real or imagined. For babies, security means the physical presence of parents' bodies.

Recently, child development specialists have begun to question the routine isolation of babies from their parents at night. They cite medical and anthropological studies that suggest continuous physical contact between parent and baby both day and night is healthy and can even be life-saving for the baby. "Isolated sleeping is not natural for the human infant," says Dr. Melvin J. Konner, a psychiatrist and anthropologist at Emory University, in an article in the *Boston Globe*. "In all known human societies other than our own Western, industrialized culture, the mother and infant sleep in the same bed," he notes. "The same is true of our closest nonhuman relatives, monkeys and chimps."[45]

Isolating babies at night is a relatively novel idea. Of 90 nonindustrialized societies surveyed in 1971, not a single one expected its babies to sleep alone. For virtually all of human history, babies have had their mothers close at night. "Primitive people rarely let their newborn child out of sight or out of contact at any time," notes Dr. Lewis P. Lipsitt, a developmental psychologist at Brown University. "I think that is a more natural way of life for humans," he says.

Psychologists have long known that frequent touch and motion stimulate growth and improve the breathing patterns of premature babies. Those who have been frequently touched, massaged, and rocked show markedly better growth than those left alone in their incubators without such stimulation. Full-term babies, too, who are held or carried by their parents show more rapid advances in their motor skills and cognitive development, and the effects can be measured many years later.[47]

Sleeping with parents may help to provide babies who have breathing problems with what could be called a "system override." All babies occasionally stop breathing for brief periods as they sleep, but some are vulnerable to longer, life-threatening episodes of apnea, or breathing cessation. This may be a cause of Sudden Infant Death Syndrome (SIDS). SIDS deaths most frequently occur when babies are sleeping in a room away from parents.

There is thought to be a crucial transition period in a baby's breathing. A primitive automatic breathing system, controlled by the lower region of the brain, changes over to a more voluntary, controlled breathing system operated by a higher and more sophisticated part of the brain. This happens sometime between the second and fourth months after birth—the peak period for SIDS. During this critical transition period, babies who have a yet unidentified central nervous system defect may be at risk for SIDS. What actually causes the breathing stoppage—whether it arises from the baby's heart, his respiratory system, or his brain—is not yet known.

Research by Dr. James J. McKenna, an anthropologist and psychologist at Pomona College in California, shows that babies and their parents influence one another's waking and breathing patterns. When mothers and their infants sleep together, McKenna found, the mothers naturally imitate their babies' pauses until both mother and baby resume breathing in unison. The parent's breathing and chest movements appear to help regularize the baby's breathing, to remind him to start breathing when he stops.[48] In a similar study, researchers at the University of Connecticut found that premature babies who sleep with a teddy bear equipped to "breathe" have more regular breathing patterns than babies who sleep alone.

Before your baby was born, he was sleeping with you every night, gently being held by your body and listening to your breathing. Some babies can be weaned from this at birth without complaining, but most babies need a more gradual weaning. They are frightened and insecure when suddenly they are expected to sleep in a cold, silent crib all alone."

DEBORAH BOEHLE
"When Babies Cry"[49]

Shared Sleep Is Good for Parents, Too

Ironically, the very thing that most parents do to get more sleep results in their getting *less* sleep. Typically, parents decide that they can sleep better if the baby is in another place, and so they put the baby in a crib in a separate room. The baby becomes frightened by the isolation and cries out to bring the parents close. A parent, aroused from sleep by the crying, gets up and feeds the baby, who goes to sleep in the parent's arms. The parent returns the baby to the crib and goes back to the other bedroom to sleep. The baby sleeps until hunger pangs and loneliness arouse him again. The baby cries, the parent is aroused, and so the night passes.

Instead of getting more sleep, the parent actually gets less sleep this way than if the baby were within arm's reach. A breastfeeding

COMMON OBJECTIONS TO SLEEPING WITH THE BABY

"He will turn out to be a homosexual."	If this were true, then 90 percent of the world's population would be homosexual. In most human societies, as in virtually all mammalian species, babies normally sleep with their mothers.
"She will smother in the blankets."	Babies can breathe adequately through blankets and quilts. They protect their faces instinctively by batting down coverings. (But don't use a waterbed or beanbag chair; these can suffocate babies.)
"My husband will roll over on her."	Some fathers do sleep heavily, but babies have the self-saving abilities to cry, kick, squirm, and move themselves if they have to.
"The baby will spoil our love life."	Put yourself between Dad and the baby so you can cuddle both. Most couples find other places for their togetherness when they allow the bed to belong to the family.
"She will mess up the bed and spit up on it."	Probably true. You can use waterproof pads, diaper covers, and mattress covers, or keep towels handy. Bedding can be washed, anyway.
"I can't sleep with the baby next to me. She keeps me awake."	It may take a while to get used to your small nighttime companion, but most parents report that waking up with their babies is a luxury.
"My partner doesn't want it. He says he needs his sleep."	Caring for a baby is as demanding as a professional job, if not more so. You need your sleep, too.

mother can nurse her baby without getting up or even waking fully. She need not sit up waiting for the baby to finally fall back into a deep sleep. And many parents have found that sleeping with their babies decreases the frequency of night wakings, so the parents themselves get more rest.

You can test this idea yourself by taking your baby into bed with you for a few nights to see if his night waking and crying are reduced. You may want to make some notes on his behavior first, so you can accurately compare his sleep patterns in isolation and in your bed.

By giving in to your baby's inborn need for closeness, you may find that you not only help him conserve his energies for emotional and physical growth, but you conserve your own energies as well.

Crib and Bed Dangers

Each year cribs are responsible for hundreds of babies' deaths, and for approximately 13 thousand injuries serious enough to require emergency room treatment. Most of the deaths occur when a baby's body slips through the bars of a broken crib but his head stays behind, so that he strangles. Strangulation happens, too, when a baby gets the neck of his T-shirt or gown, or a pacifier string, caught around a fancy crib post or cutout. New federal safety standards have helped to lower the number of infant deaths, but fatal accidents are still happening with older, malfunctioning or poorly designed cribs.

Over twenty babies in the United States have died face down in waterbeds and beanbag chairs. Typically, the baby is unable to lift his head high enough to prevent suffocation when his face is buried in a nonbreathable surface, such as a plastic waterbed mattress or the pocket created around a baby's face in a plastic-surfaced beanbag chair. Babies die, too, when their faces get trapped in plastic bags parents have put around mattresses.

More rarely, babies become entrapped and strangle between the headboards and poorly fitting mattresses or broken springs of conventional beds, or between the bed and furniture next to the bed, such as a night stand. Most often these accidents happen when parents have left the baby to sleep alone.

Should you decide to sleep with your baby, remove the mattress from the bed frame and place it directly on the floor. There will be no danger of entrapment beside the bed's headboard or any other hard surface, and you won't have to worry about the baby being hurt from a fall.

"You don't put a baby who doesn't sleep well in a crib, you put him in the bed with you. Just throw your crib away and buy a new dress. Once he's asleep, don't move him. Once you move him, that's it!"

Some parents bring their baby's crib into their bedroom, and remove one of the sides so it fits flush against the side of the bed (the crib mattress may need to be lowered to its lowest position). This arrangement makes it easy to move the baby back and forth between beds. It is critical to tie the crib frame securely to the bed frame so there will never be a gap between the two mattresses.

Providing a safe and secure environment for your baby can help you both sleep better.

CHAPTER FOUR

Your Guide to Successful Feeding

YOUR BABY'S FACE AND MOUTH structure are ideally suited for breastfeeding. Her short, upturned nose and flared nostrils enable her to breathe while nursing. Her flexible chin is designed to operate like a tiny pile driver, jamming into the breast to stimulate the milk letdown. Her receding lower jaw can rotate to compress the milk ducts situated an inch or so in back of your nipple, while her padded cheeks create a firm vacuum chamber that holds your breast in place.

It may take a while for your newborn baby to coordinate her latching on, tonguing, and jaw actions, but her inborn reflexes help. She comes equipped with a powerful rooting reflex that will cause her to automatically turn in the direction of your touch on her cheek. And if your nipple tickles her lower lip, she is likely to open her mouth wide like a hungry baby bird to receive your breast.

The most important part of your baby's anatomy for feeding is her tongue. She doesn't simply *suck* milk from your nipple—she uses her jaws to compress milk sinuses and the undulations of her tongue to cup breast tissue and press it against the roof of her mouth. When milk sprays from your nipple, her tongue drops down, forming a channel for collecting and swallowing.

In the first few days after birth, your breasts will produce a special substance called *colostrum*, which acts as a high-protein meal and laxative to help clean out the sticky, dark meconium that you'll soon find in your baby's diaper. It will probably take a few days for your milk flow to start.

Human milk looks and tastes different from cow's milk. It's thinner, more watery, and sweeter. During each feeding, the composition of your milk gradually changes from less fatty foremilk to creamier hindmilk. To get an adequate balance of both foremilk and hindmilk, your baby needs to completely finish nursing on the first breast before being switched over to the second. You'll know she's through when she releases your breast.

Unless your baby is sluggish and sleepy from anesthesia or pain relievers you've taken, she will probably be alert during the first few hours after birth, and ready to nurse some time during this period (though not necessarily just after delivery). If you keep your baby with you from birth onward, you can respond quickly when she signals she is ready—by nuzzling you, sucking her fist, or starting to fret. After this period of alertness, most babies fall into a deep sleep and don't awaken again for three to four hours. If the baby's initial readiness to nurse is ignored, eagerness can turn into stupor or extreme irritability. If nursing is delayed too long, the mother's breasts may become painfully engorged—swollen and hard.

Nursing your baby right away makes your milk come in more quickly. A study of one hundred breastfeeding mothers found that the twenty-eight who put their babies to their breasts soon after birth lactated earlier than those who did not nurse their babies until later. The thirteen mothers whose milk came in on the first and second day after birth had suckled immediately. Mothers who received no drugs during birth, also, lactated earlier than those who were medicated.[50]

Beware the Bottle

Be forewarned that babies are often fed glucose (sugar) water or formula in hospital nurseries. As many as 95 percent of breastfeeding babies adopt an abnormal mouthing action from being introduced to the bottle in the first weeks after birth. A bottle-fed baby learns to clamp down to keep milk from coming too fast, to use her tongue as a stopper, or to hold her lips in a contracted, tight ring. Any of these patterns will interfere with a baby's ability to milk the breast effectively. Giving a baby bottles also fills her up so she is less interested in nursing. And if the baby is prone to allergies, giving formula can sometimes cause severe reactions to cow's milk later on. When you're in the hospital, be sure all the nurses know that you'll feed the baby whenever she fusses, and that you don't want her to have bottles or pacifiers.

Positioning Is Important

You may notice that your nipples have a tender, "sunburned" feeling after your baby's first few feedings. This happens when the nipples get stretched into long, ribbon-like shapes by your baby's tongue. If nipple pain and soreness continue beyond the first few days, check your positioning.

The most common way to position a baby for nursing is the cradle hold. The baby lies on one of your arms, her head resting in the crook of your elbow. She faces you, tummy to tummy. You can grasp her bottom or thigh with your hand. Avoid putting pressure on the back of your baby's head, because this could frustrate her need to position herself.

If you're sitting up in bed, you may want to place a pillow behind your back, one under your baby to help support her, and one under your knees. If you're in a chair, sit up straight, and use pillows in your lap to help support the baby. You may want to use a footstool.

The football hold is helpful if you've had a cesarean section or your baby appears to have trouble latching on. Sit the baby up along your side so that her face is near your breast. Position a pillow under her to bring her up to your nipple. Use your arm to support her back, and your hands to hold her neck. Use pillows behind your shoulders to increase your comfort.

Lying on your side is an especially restful nursing position, and the one you're most likely to use at night. You may want to elevate your newborn a bit by laying her on a pillow.

In any of these positions, cup your free hand beneath your breast so that your thumb rests on the top, about an inch or so above your areola. Tickle the baby's lower lip with your nipple, or express a little milk on it so that she opens her mouth wide, as if she's yawning. Then put as much of your breast into her mouth as you can. The baby should take in most of your areola (the colored ring around your nipple). Her lips should flange outward around the breast, and her tongue should be positioned between the underside of your breast and her lower gum line.

If your baby has developed an altered nursing pattern after being given a bottle, you may need help in getting her to change. Your nurse or midwife may be able to guide you, or perhaps she can refer you to a lactation consultant in your area. Breastfeeding counseling is also available from La Leche League, a national organization whose

> *"Show me a mother with really sore nipples, and I'll show you a fussy baby who's not milking the breast properly. Have you ever tried to eat or drink while facing sideways? That's just the way that many mothers try to make their babies nurse."*
>
> KITTIE FRANTZ
> Director
> Breastfeeding Infant Clinic[51]

local phone number should be listed in your phone book (or call 800-LA LECHE toll-free). The Nursing Mothers Counsel provides breastfeeding assistance in California, Colorado, Indiana, and Georgia; call 415-591-6688 for a local number.

Let Your Baby Regulate Your Milk Production

Some people may advise you to limit the time your baby nurses at a breast, or to make sure a certain amount of time passes between feedings. Thank them for the advice, then forget it.

The most important principle of breastfeeding is this: **How much milk your body produces depends on how much stimulation your breasts get.** So if you put your baby on a schedule of nursing only every four hours, for example, your breasts may not produce enough milk for her.

Beyond the first three or four days after birth, most newborns need to nurse eight to twelve times in a twenty-four-hour day. How often and how long your baby nurses depends on her own unique needs; what's right for one baby may not be right for another. Your baby may want to nurse for hours at a time and then sleep, or she may nurse for only a few minutes at a time, with shorter periods between feedings.

As your baby becomes more skilled at nursing, she will drain your breasts faster, and your milk production will gradually increase to match her needs. Except during the natural milk-building phases (see page 48), she will probably nurse less frequently and for shorter intervals as time passes.

Are You Making Enough Milk?

Often new mothers worry that they aren't making enough milk. After all, nursing is not like bottle feeding—you can't watch the ounces go in. Believe it or not, though, once milk-making is well established your baby may get 19 to 20 ounces of milk a day—and by the time she reaches six months she'll get almost 30 ounces of milk a day!

If you are worried that your baby may not be getting enough milk, listen for her swallowing—"uhhh . . . hhuh . . . uck." When you hear these sounds you know she is downing milk. You can also reassure yourself by counting diaper changes. Your baby should thoroughly wet at least six to eight cloth diapers (or five to six disposables) every twenty-four hours, and by the fourth or fifth day her stools should be starting to turn from black to yellow. If all this is happening, the baby is probably getting enough milk.

The time to worry is when your baby is not gaining weight as she should. It is normal for a baby to lose weight after birth, but then to regain her birth weight by two weeks of age and to continue gaining approximately an ounce a day after that. For your own reassurance, have your baby weighed at two weeks of age. If she has reached or surpassed her birth weight, you'll know everything is progressing normally. And if slow weight gain is going to be a problem, you'll get an early start on dealing with it.

The Let-Down Response

At some point during the first two months, you will probably begin to experience the feeling of your milk letting down. You may feel pressure or fullness in your breasts, along with a tingling, pins-and-needles sensation. Your milk may start to drip or spray, and you may experience an overall feeling of relaxation.

Mothers don't have just one letdown during a feeding, but one or two large ones followed by a cascade of smaller ones. In time, you'll see that your baby's sucking patterns change according to your letdowns. At first she will suck rapidly, as if to prime the pump; then, as the letdown comes, her jaw will drop down, and her sucks will become longer and more deliberate.

Some mothers find that the first letdown of a feeding is too powerful for their babies to handle. The baby sucks and sucks to make the milk come, and then, *whoosh!*, the milk sprays out so fast that she struggles to swallow without choking. She may take in air, which can lead to belly pain.

One way to deal with an overactive letdown is to take the baby off the breast when you feel the milk coming. Gently break your baby's suction by pressing your pinky between the side of her mouth and your breast. Let the initial gush flow into a diaper or a washcloth for a moment, then put the baby back on. Another way is to lie back at a 45-degree angle while nursing, with the baby on top of you. This way the extra milk can dribble off without choking the baby. In time your baby will adapt to your body's letdown style.

"*Basic trust that when you're hungry you're going to be fed is clearly important. But I think one of the things that's most basic and important to a baby is being understood.*"

DR. DANIEL STERN
Author, *Diary of a Baby*[53]

How to Orchestrate a Good Feeding

Whether you elect to totally breastfeed your baby, to give her supplemental formula, or to feed her only formula, there are certain feeding strategies you can use to help reduce fussiness at mealtimes. Surveys show that both breastfed and bottle-fed babies are more likely to be fussy at feeding time than at any other time during the day.

One major cause of mealtime fussiness is simply *hunger*. Rigid scheduling is usually the problem. Parents are sometimes instructed to feed their babies only every three to four hours, but your baby may need to be fed more often. When she cries from hunger, you may glance at your watch and decide it's not time yet. She begins to get really upset, even frantic. Her hunger cries develop into full-blown pain cries. Finally, when you offer her food, she's sobbing. She chokes and swallows a lot of air. Her belly feels tied in a knot, and it hurts. No wonder mealtime has become such a hassle! The cure is simple: Feed your baby when she seems hungry and not by a preset schedule.

If your baby is upset for any reason, trying to nurse her out of a long crying jag is a quick ticket to baby indigestion. She can't nurse well when her stomach is tight and her breathing is out of rhythm. Ina May Gaskin, a midwife and the author of *Spiritual Midwifery*, suggests that you help your baby to relax before a feeding by tapping her on the cheek while softly talking with her.[52]

Your baby may be tense at feeding time partially because *you* are. Babies are very aware of tension signals from their parents. They respond to cues such as a mother's smell, breathing, facial expressions, and muscle tone. To help ensure relaxing mealtimes, create a cozy, secluded place expressly for feeding. Start with a rocking chair or other comfortable chair. Add a footstool if it makes you more comfortable. Turn off the radio and TV. Unplug the phone, or turn on the answering machine so you won't be tempted to answer any calls. Get yourself a drink, and put it on the table beside you. Turn on a recording of restful music. Tell yourself that you've got all day to feed your baby, if that's what it takes.

Then consciously relax yourself. Nestle your baby against you. Take a few deep breaths as you soften the muscles of your arms and your abdomen. Keep yourself still. Silently watch your baby, being careful not to interrupt her natural suck-pause-suck rhythms with your touches, your movements, or talking. (See "Practicing Dynamic Relaxation," pages 133–38, for suggestions about how to relax.)

TIPS FOR BETTER FEEDINGS

✔ Set up a feeding nest with support pillows, a footstool, something for you to drink, and an extra diaper.

✔ Since your baby interprets abrupt handling as a signal of danger, try picking her up in slow motion, and changing her positions gracefully and smoothly.

✔ If your newborn is sleepy, awaken her fully before a feeding. Unwrap her, and change her diaper if it is wet.

✔ Sit her up, talk to her, and pat or rub her back before attempting to nurse her.

✔ Fasten your baby's diaper loosely before the meal so that it doesn't press into her belly.

✔ Since your baby interprets tension in your arms and belly as a sign to hurry or worry, train yourself to relax them into cushiony softness.

✔ If your baby is upset, help her to relax a little before you feed her. Tap her gently on the cheek and talk to her soothingly while looking her in the eye. Settle her down into your arms. Drip a drop or two of milk on her lips before you start.

✔ Consciously slow and deepen your breathing. Regardless of how tense you feel, this may help your baby release her own tension.

✔ Rock the baby gently while feeding her to relax both of you and to help the milk coat her stomach evenly.

✔ Rather than patting or jiggling the baby to bring up a burp, lay her on her right side for a moment and then gently bring her into an upright position against your shoulder.

✔ Let your baby nap in a semi-upright position, in an infant seat or car seat, rather than laying her down flat.

"Sometimes parents try too hard," notes Dr. Tiffany Field, of the Mailman Center for Child Development in Miami, Florida, who has carefully observed hundreds of parents feeding babies. "It reminds

"At first I had a hard time telling if my baby was awake or asleep. If I jumped up to feed him on his first whimpers, I sometimes would find myself trying to nurse a semiconscious baby who was only halfheartedly trying to eat. An hour or so later he'd be awake and really wanting to nurse. Now I wait to be sure he's really awake and really hungry first."

me of when people mistakenly try to communicate with a foreigner by yelling louder and faster rather than slowing down." These parents move the nipple a lot, rub the baby's head or face, and coax her to keep on drinking. In doing so, they are failing to recognize her need to concentrate. She turns her head away, arches her back, bats at the breast or bottle, or gags. Ina May Gaskin offers this solution:

> Sometimes I'll see a mother breastfeeding her new baby and while the baby is sucking, she'll be rubbing her fingers back and forth on his leg, feeling how soft he is, or maybe plucking at his toes, marvelling how tiny they are, and all the time she is fussing with his body—she's not realizing that this is the same as tapping on someone's shoulder trying to get their attention while they're trying to make love. I have cured several babies of colic by pointing out to the mother that the way she was handling the baby while he nursed made his stomach and intestines uptight and caused cramps. Once she learned to get a nice firm grip on his thigh or his butt and let him know she was there without touch-talking irrelevant things to him while they made love—which is what breastfeeding is, after all—then the baby would get over his bellyache.[54]

A newborn may fall asleep soon after beginning a feeding, and it may take a while to awaken her enough to nurse. New parents sometimes keep right on feeding a baby and talking to her after she has drifted off. Usually the baby will let go of the nipple upon falling asleep, but sometimes she may not. Then, if the milk keeps coming, she wakes up abruptly, sputtering and confused. After a while, parents learn that when a baby's breathing deepens and her limbs go limp, it is time to end the feeding, or to gently stir her awake by touching the nipple to her lips or by jostling her. If your newborn is persistently sleepy, make sure you fully awaken her before beginning a feeding: unwrap and undress her, tap her on the foot, or put a damp cloth on her forehead.

Don't Rush to Wean

Baby formula advertisers are very cunning in trying to persuade breastfeeding mothers that babies need supplemental bottles. **Your own milk provides excellent nutrition for your baby's first six months.** Giving your baby supplemental formula or solids in the early months will cause your baby to nurse less often and for shorter periods—clear signals to your body to cut back on milk production. Introducing other foods too early may also cause allergic reactions, which only increase fussiness.

Babies naturally go through appetite spurts, often at two to three weeks, then again around six weeks and twelve weeks. During these times you may find yourself nursing nearly around the clock for three to four days in a row. But don't take your baby's demands as a signal to start weaning or offering solids. She is just stimulating your milk production to keep up with her rapid growth.

Teething pain and oncoming illnesses can also spark nursing binges. It's easy to get short-tempered about suddenly being so much in demand, but reassure yourself that you are giving your baby what she needs, for her emotional as well as physical well-being.

Sometimes when a mother tells her physician that her breastfed baby is fussy, the doctor jumps to the conclusion that breastfeeding is to blame, rather than thoroughly screening the baby for physical causes of pain. Most physicians, lacking training about breastfeeding, are unfamiliar with common problems that cause nursing difficulties. They may not know, for example, how to examine a nursing mother's breasts and nipples, or how to tell if a baby isn't positioned or latching on properly.

If your physician suggests that you try giving your fussy baby formula—beware! This could cause a baby sensitive to cow's milk to have an allergic reaction and thus become even more fussy. Although shifting a baby from mother's milk to cow's milk may temporarily lessen a baby's crying, even worse fussiness may set in a week to ten days later. By then, sadly, a mother has gone through a painful process of engorgement and drying up, while her baby has become committed to a long cycle of trying one formula after another, all of which may fail to help her get better. Gradual weaning based on your baby's signals is physically and psychologically better for you and your baby.

That your newborn is irritable is not by itself a reason to conclude that something is wrong with your milk. You might say to your physician, *"I am not convinced that breastfeeding is the problem here. Have we explored every other possibility?"* (For help in determining the reasons for your baby's discomfort, see chapter 7, "The Colic-Allergy Connection," and chapter 8, "Doctors, Disease, and Drugs.") If you and your baby *do* have a feeding problem, you can probably solve it with the help of a volunteer from La Leche League or the Nursing Mothers Counsel (see pages 41–42) or a professional lactation consultant.

"Take all magical solutions with a grain of salt. Just because putting Johnny on formula seemed to help him doesn't mean you should go out and wean your baby. Relatives are often quick to present the magical solutions that are the least helpful."

CAUSES OF FUSSINESS AT THE BREAST

PROBLEM	DESCRIPTION	SOLUTION
Engorgement	Your nipples have become too difficult to grasp because your breasts are swollen with milk. This happens when the milk comes in, and later from insufficient nursing or from poor positioning.	Express enough milk from your breast so your baby can latch on. Allow your baby to nurse as long and as often as she wants. After nursing, apply cool compresses. Avoid supplements, which reduce a baby's appetite and cause "nipple confusion."
Overstrong letdown	Your baby latches on and sucks, but suddenly begins to choke, which causes her to release the breast.	Remove the baby from the breast. Allow some of the milk to spray out into a diaper, then offer the baby the breast again.
Nonstop nursing	The baby wants to nurse almost constantly.	Before your milk comes in this is normal behavior; it helps to establish the milk flow. Allow the baby to nurse as often and long as she wants. If the baby wants to nurse nonstop after milk comes in, your positioning may be affecting her ability to completely drain the breast. Make certain that (1) you are holding the baby tummy to tummy, (2) the baby has enough breast tissue in her mouth, (3) her tongue is positioned over her lower gum. At 2 to 3 weeks, 6 weeks, and about 12 weeks, an appetite spurt is normal; your baby nurses more to increase milk production. If nonstop nursing continues although the baby is gaining weight well, try alternative soothing methods. A baby may suck and suck when she really needs to burp, is going to have a bowel movement, or is experiencing some other discomfort.
Foremilk-hindmilk imbalance	Your baby is getting too much foremilk, causing a lactose (milk sugar) overload. This may result in gas, diarrhea, and discomfort.	Don't switch the baby from one breast to the other before she completely empties and releases the first one. You might try nursing at only one breast per feeding.

CAUSES OF FUSSINESS AT THE BREAST—*Continued*

PROBLEM	DESCRIPTION	SOLUTION

Insufficient milk	Your breasts are producing too little milk, probably because of inadequate stimulation. This could be due to (1) poor positioning, (2) too brief or infrequent nursing, or (3) the baby's sucking problems.
	
	    Rarer causes: Milk production can be affected by a mother's (1) high blood pressure, (2) thyroid condition, (3) severe emotional distress, or (4) intake of drugs that affect milk production (see page 56).
		To check if your baby is getting sufficient milk: (1) Weigh the baby. Most babies lose weight at first but regain their birth weight within two to three weeks, and put on 4 to 8 ounces per week thereafter for the first six months. (2) Count wet diapers. At least 6 to 8 thoroughly wet cloth diapers (4 to 6 disposables) per day mean the baby is getting enough fluids.
		
		    Consult a lactation consultant or breastfeeding counselor if underfeeding is the problem.

Flat or inverted nipples	Your baby has trouble grasping your nipple because it is flat, or it folds into the areola when it's compressed.	Wear a breast shell under your bra, or cut a nipple-sized hole out of the bra so your nipple protrudes.*
		
		    Before nursing, pull on the nipple a few times, or apply a cold compress to make it stand out.
		
		    Pinch a flat nipple so the baby can latch on. If the nipple is inverted, push your breast against your chest, your thumb and fingers surrounding the areola.
		
		    Use the football hold (see page 41).

Poor mouthing, tonguing, or jaw action	Some newborns have difficulty coordinating nursing; they use their tongues or lips incorrectly. This may be due to developmental delays, especially if the baby is premature. Or the baby may be tongue-tied; the string-like frenulum under the tongue may be too short or too close to the tip of the tongue.	Try alternative positions, such as the football hold (see page 41).
		
		    If the baby's tongue is positioned too far back in her mouth, massage it down and forward with your finger before nursing.
		
		    If the baby is tongue-tied, ask a doctor to clip the frenulum. This is a simple and quick procedure.
		
		    Seek help from a lactation consultant, a breastfeeding counselor, or a physical or occupational therapist specializing in infants.

Continued on next page

CAUSES OF FUSSINESS AT THE BREAST—*Continued*

PROBLEM	DESCRIPTION	SOLUTION
Food allergies (see chapter 7)	Your baby may be sensitive to something in your diet. Symptoms in the baby may include diarrhea, green, frothy stools, gas, rash, and a stuffy or runny nose.	Try eliminating allergenic foods from your diet (see pages 85–91).
Thrush (see page 99)	A yeast infection in the baby's mouth may make nursing uncomfortable for her. A baby with thrush has white, cheesy-looking patches in her mouth. She may also have a diaper rash that doesn't go away, and your nipples may be reddened and itchy or burning.	Thrush is easily treated with liquid nystatin, which must be prescribed by a doctor. Your nipples should be treated at the same time; nystatin ointment is usually prescribed.

*This suggestion is from S. M. Maher, *An Overview of Solutions to Breastfeeding and Sucking Problems* (Franklin Park, Ill.: La Leche League International), p. 5.

Burping, Spitting Up, and Vomiting

Burping is letting up air, and it can make a baby feel more comfortable. Sometimes you can hear the air going down. If your baby is really hungry, she may continue crying and trying to nurse at the same time. If this happens, it's best to stop feeding and put her upright for a moment; otherwise, she may only keep swallowing air and finally spit up everything.

Sometimes parents take burping too seriously, and interrupt a feeding over and over in the hope of getting up an air bubble. But there's really no reason for breaking into a peaceful feeding just to hear a "b-u-r-p." You have to feel sorry for babies who don't get to drink in peace, but get patted, jiggled, and shaken every few minutes so their parents (or grandparents) can be reassured by that sound.

If your baby seems content, it's better to wait until she has finished at one breast, or finished the bottle, before laying her on your shoulder or sitting her up briefly to bring up air. If she stops sucking to cry, carry her around in an upright position for a while. The burp will eventually come, and then she can resume the feeding, if she doesn't fall asleep in the meantime.

REASONS FOR CONTINUING TO BREASTFEED YOUR FUSSY BABY

BENEFIT	DESCRIPTION	HOW TO EXPLAIN YOUR DECISION
Immunities	Because of the antibodies in human milk, breastfed babies have fewer respiratory infections, bouts of diarrhea, and life-threatening illnesses. Immunities continue throughout the first year of life or longer.	*"I want to offer my baby maximum protection from illnesses."*
Oral development	Breastfed children develop less tooth decay than those who are bottle-fed, with or without fluoridation. Breastfed babies are also less likely to develop problems with abnormal tongue thrusting and jaw alignment, which could lead to speech impairments.	*"I want to ensure better oral development for my baby."*
Fewer ear infections	Breastfed babies tend to have fewer ear infections than bottle-fed babies.	*"I hope to protect my baby from chronic ear infections."*
Insurance against obesity	Breastfed babies are less likely to be obese in childhood, adolescence, and adulthood.	*"I want to reduce the chances of my child growing up obese."*
Emotional satisfaction	Breastfeeding babies experience more physical and emotional intimacy with their mothers, which helps them to grow up into confident, independent children and adults.	*"I want to provide the closeness my baby needs to feel secure, particularly when she is experiencing discomfort."*

Don't confuse swallowed air with what comes out the other end as gas. The walls of a baby's intestines normally absorb extra air during digestion. If your baby has a lot of gurgling in her belly and is expelling a lot of gas, she may be reacting to something in her formula, or to something in your diet that is reaching her through your milk. (See chapter 7, "The Colic-Allergy Connection.")

Spitting up is a very normal part of babyhood. Some babies spit up frequently; others don't. Typically, a baby looks smilingly content just before she spits up a little or a lot of her last meal all over your best shirt. Sometimes the spit-up just rolls out the corner of her mouth, and she seems unaware anything has happened. The stomach contents may be odorless, sour-smelling, or curdled. Some babies may spit up a dozen times a day—yet they gain weight and seem perfectly healthy. Fortunately, spitting up usually stops by the time a baby gets up on her own two feet.

Spitting up may be due to a lax *cardiac sphincter,* at the esophagus end of the stomach. When the stomach contracts to empty, the *pyloric sphincter* at the opposite end of the stomach opens to let food pass into the small intestine—but the cardiac sphincter may open at the same time, allowing some of the milk to squirt back up and be spit up. To help prevent this, hold your baby upright for a few minutes after feeding, and avoid excess motion. You may find that your baby spits up less when lying down if she is placed on her right side.

One cause of spitting up is overfeeding—your baby cries after you feed her, and nothing seems to soothe her, so in desperation you feed her again. She cries more and spits up, or even throws up. Be cautious about putting food on top of food just because your baby fusses. Once I watched a nervous mother feed her baby one bottle after another during an airline flight to keep him from crying. Everything was fine until about fifteen minutes before landing, when the baby threw up what looked like a quart of milk all down his mommy's blouse and suit. A pacifier or his mother's pinky finger, pad side up, would have worked better. See chapter 2, "The Best Ways to Deal with Crying," for alternative soothing techniques.

If your breastfed baby fusses and spits up continually yet is gaining weight faster than the norm, she may be getting too much foremilk in relation to hindmilk. Be sure you are letting her suck to satisfaction at one breast before switching her to the other. Some babies are actually happier nursing on only one side per feeding.

Vomiting differs from spitting up in that the stomach contents are forcefully thrown out. Most babies vomit occasionally, for various reasons. Gulping rapidly, swallowing a lot of air without burping, excessive jostling, and allergies are all possible causes of vomiting. Vomiting caused by an allergy is usually accompanied by gas and diarrhea, and sometimes by an incessantly stuffy or runny nose. (See chapter 7, "The Colic-Allergy Connection.")

Sometimes a baby's vomiting is so forceful that it is called *projectile vomiting.* Unimpeded, the stomach contents might travel halfway across the room! As long as this happens only once in a while, your baby seems active, happy, and otherwise healthy, and she has a good appetite, there is no cause for concern. But if your baby vomits every day, has frequent projectile vomiting, or chokes and coughs a lot after spitting up or vomiting, you should notify your physician right away. Your baby may have a serious physical problem, such as a blockage in her digestive system or severe gastroesophageal reflux (see "Rarer Causes of Feeding Problems," page 58).

Feeding and Thumb Sucking

Babies' natural drive to suck serves functions beyond just getting milk into them. They suck fingers, fists, thumbs, or pacifiers to soothe themselves and gain some self-control in the face of hunger, fatigue, or discomfort. After a feeding, a baby may keep sucking to help herself through an episode of stomach bloating or belly pain.

Chances are your baby will abandon finger and thumb sucking sometime in the first year, but some children keep sucking their thumbs until they're six or seven years old. To understand why, researchers compared the histories of fifty habitual thumb suckers, aged one to seven years, with the histories of a similar group of children who did not suck their thumbs. It was found that the amount of time a baby was allowed to suck at the breast or bottle appeared to have no effect on later thumb sucking. But babies put on rigid feeding schedules were more likely to become thumb-suckers than those who were fed whenever they were hungry. And the way babies were put to sleep appeared to be crucial in establishing long-term thumb-sucking habits. *Ninety-six percent of the habitual thumb-suckers had been left to fall asleep alone after feedings.*[55]

Among the children who were allowed to suck at the breast or bottle while going to sleep, in bed or in their parents' arms, not a single one turned out to be a long-term finger- or thumb-sucker. If you feed your baby on demand and nurse her to sleep, then there is no need to worry that she'll grow into a thumb-sucking six-year-old.

Drugs and Breast Milk

Since almost any drug you take while breastfeeding will reach your baby, you will certainly want to avoid taking unnecessary medications. But perhaps you have a medical condition that necessitates treatment with a drug. It may be that you'll have to stop nursing, at least temporarily. Then again, the drug may not reach the milk in amounts great enough to do your baby harm.

For any particular medication, you'll want to know how long it has been in use, particularly with infants or nursing mothers. Have any adverse reactions been reported? Is this a new drug, whose possible side effects are little known?

If a drug has been in use for many years, the risks it poses to a

"It is widely recognized that nearly all maternally administered drugs and environmental chemicals find their way to the breastfeeding infant."

DR. NEIL K. KOCHENOUR
AND
DR. MAURICE G. EMERY[57]

breastfed baby are probably well documented. But with newer drugs, we must rely on researchers' rather than consumers' reports. Most drugs, in fact, fall into a "gray area"—researchers differ in their conclusions about how much of the drug reaches the mother's milk and how the drug affects the nursing baby. Research on breast milk has pitfalls. For example, if researchers measure drug amounts only in the mothers' first letdowns, then drugs that characteristically bind themselves to the fatty hindmilk are not accurately assessed. Effects on babies may be assessed differently, too, since there are no industry standards about what constitutes a baby's adverse reaction.

You'll also want to consider your baby's age, how long you must take the medication, and how long it persists in the body. If your baby is very young she will have an especially hard time metabolizing foreign chemicals. If the drug is long-acting, accumulating in your body and the baby's, it will pose even more risk to your baby's health, particularly if you must continue the treatment over a long period. But if the drug is quickly eliminated from the body, you may be able to coordinate feedings and doses to minimize the amount that reaches the baby.

Drugs ingested through breast milk can affect babies in various ways. Common reactions include diarrhea, crying, and fussiness. Some drugs may harm a baby in ways that are not immediately evident; hormones, steroids, and certain antibiotics are among these. For example, penicillin administered to a breastfeeding mother has been linked in some instances to her child's severe allergic reactions to the antibiotic later on. (Other antibiotics are less likely to pose this risk.) A few drugs known to affect babies are listed in the chart "Some Drugs That Affect Babies through Breast Milk." A more detailed list is included in Kathleen Huggins's *Nursing Mother's Companion*.[56]

Even if a drug poses no direct risk to your baby, it may interfere with your milk-making process. It may reduce the volume of milk you produce, alter the protein composition of the milk, interfere with your letdown, or sedate you, dulling your sensitivity to your baby's signals. Such drugs are particularly dangerous if taken in high doses or over an extended period. Some of them are listed in the chart "Drugs That Affect Milk Supply."

SOME DRUGS THAT AFFECT BABIES THROUGH BREAST MILK

DRUG NAME	POSSIBLE EFFECTS ON BABY
Ampicillin	Diarrhea and (rarely) later allergic reactions.
Antihistamines	Drowsiness.
Decongestants	Those containing the chemical phenyl-propanolamine (including Allerest, Contac, 4-Way Nasal Spray, Sine-Off, Sinutab, Triaminic, Triaminicol, and Tussagesic) may cause night crying and irritability.
Laxatives	Those containing phenolphthalein, cascara, or aloe may cause diarrhea.
Sedatives and sleep medications	All can cause drowsiness; some may cause dependence and withdrawal.
Migraine headache medications	Those containing ergotamine may cause symptoms from vomiting and diarrhea to weak pulse and unstable blood pressure.

Tips for Bottle Feeding

Physical closeness between you and your baby is of utmost importance whether your baby is breast- or bottle-fed. While bottle feeding, then, use the breastfeeding relationship as your model. Hold the baby in your arms or beside you in the bed during every feeding, and let her fall asleep against you. This will help her to relax, secure in your love and protection.

The bottle should be positioned for feeding at a 45-degree angle. Raise the end as your baby drinks so that the nipple stays filled. This will help to keep the baby from sucking air.

Which bottles or nipples you choose for your baby probably doesn't matter a lot, but glass bottles are less likely to cause allergic reactions in babies than plastic ones. If your baby gets "contact dermatitis"—a rash where plastic pants, plastic parts of disposable

Drugs That Affect Milk Supply

Kind of Drug	Generic Name	Trade Names of Medications Containing This Drug
Antispasmodics (for spasms in the stomach or lower digestive tract)	atropine (belladonna)	Contac, Donnagel, Donnatel
	dicyclomine	Bentyl, Nospaz, Triacetin
	propantheline	Norpanth, Pro-Banthine, Ropanth
	tridihexethyl	Pathilon, Milpath, Pathibamate
Lactation inhibitors (milk dry-up pills)	bromocriptine mesylate	Parlodel
	diethylstilbestrol	Stilphostrol, Tylosterone
Migraine headache medication	ergotamine	Ergomar, Ergostat, Gynergen, Bellergal, Cafergot
Allergy medications	tripelennamine	Pyribenzamine, Ro-Hist, Inhiston, Robitussin-AC, Triaminicin, Triaminicol, Tussagesic
	diphenhydramine	Benadryl, Ambrodryl, Ambenyl, Benylin
Medications for Parkinson's disease	levadopa	Bendopa, Dopar, Larodopa, Sinemet

Note: A more comprehensive listing of drugs that affect milk supply is in—American Academy of Pediatrics Committee on Drugs, "Transfer of Drugs and Other Chemicals into Human Milk," *Pediatrics* 84, no. 5 (1989):924–93.

diapers, or plastic teethers touch her skin—she may react to the tiny plastic particles that get into her milk from plastic nurser bags or bottles.[58]

Nipple shapes aren't terribly important, either. Advertisers may say their nurser nipples resemble a woman's breast nipple, but when a baby breastfeeds her mother's nipple actually stretches out into a thin ribbon-like shape, sometimes as much as an inch long, with only a small bulb at the tip end. Also, rubber is different from skin and flesh. The slender middle of a bulb-shaped "orthodontic" nipple can stick together or collapse—especially when the rubber starts to deteriorate because of poor cleaning and exposure to saliva and heat.

Traditionally shaped nipples, such as Evenflo's, with one or two holes in the tip, are probably the most reliable models to use. But experiment with several different brands, including the orthodontic kind, to see which your baby prefers. Nipples should be replaced as soon as they start to get rough and sticky.

Most manufacturers now offer nipples made of silicone as well as rubber versions. Silicone is better for the purpose than rubber—it's odorless and tasteless, and does not contain nitrosamines, cancer-causing chemicals found in rubber nipples. If you opt for rubber nipples, the Food and Drug Administration suggests that before using them you boil them for five minutes five or six times, changing the water each time, to make certain they are cleared of all chemical residues.

If the nipple holes are letting too much milk through, your baby will probably try to squeeze the nipple shut with her jaws, or she may choke. She may swallow a lot of air, causing belly pain. You'll know something's wrong when she tries to push the bottle out of her mouth again and again.

If the milk always flows too fast, your baby may learn to use her tongue as a small dam to control its flow. Some bottle-fed babies adopt a permanent tongue-thrusting habit that interferes with proper speech later on.

If the nipple holes are too small, the milk will move very slowly out of the bottle, and your baby will struggle to suck it out. The nipple may collapse from her hard sucking, and she may become frustrated and fretful.

The best way to test if the nipple holes are too big or too small is to turn the bottle upside down to watch how quickly the liquid drips out. A rapid, almost flowing drip is far too fast. A slow drip . . . drip . . . drip is more on target.

The old way to make nipple holes larger was to heat the tip of a needle with a match until the needle was red-hot, and then to insert it into the nipple holes, stretching the rubber. This method, however, could cause silicone to split or tear. Just throw away a silicone nipple that doesn't work right, and try out several new kinds to find the one your baby prefers.

Some parents take great pride in their baby's holding her own bottle, as though this were the first indication of her superior intelligence. A baby under one year of age who is lying alone and holding her own bottle is displaying not her intelligence, but her parents' neglect.

Every few years some enterprising soul comes up with yet another way to prop up a baby bottle. There are clamps that fasten to the side of the crib with long springs that attach to the bottle, inflatable bibs with snaps for the bottle, and bottles with a variety of handles—all supposedly designed to free parents so they can "do other things."

Don't fall for any of these gimmicks. Bottle propping can be dangerous. If your baby chokes or spits up, she may lose control of the milk flow so that she breathes milk into her lungs, which could

"Either the nipple hole was always too tiny and the baby couldn't get anything out, or it was too large and he choked. One night we left a nipple boiling by mistake and filled the whole apartment with silicone smoke."

cause pneumonia. Bottle propping can also make a baby more vulnerable to ear infections—especially if she drinks while lying flat on her back. In this position milk can back up into the Eustachian tube and enter the middle ear, forming a perfect medium for the growth of bacteria.

"Baby bottle mouth" is another problem that can happen when parents give a baby a bottle to take to bed, rather than holding her at feeding time. A baby's front teeth begin to decay and crumble when acids in formula and fruit juices pool around them as she sleeps. Decay shows up first as white spots on the inner side of the teeth. Then the teeth gradually turn yellow or brown. If the problem is not caught early enough, the crumbling teeth may have to be extracted to prevent decay from traveling into the permanent teeth waiting under the gums.

Rarer Causes of Feeding Problems

Many parents have told me that they knew "something just wasn't right" about their babies at feeding time, even though their pediatricians couldn't identify the baby's problem or didn't take the parents' concerns seriously.

Some babies may simply have very immature nervous systems when they're born. They may be extremely excitable, arching their backs and crying lustily when parents try to hold them and feed them. Or they may be so sleepy they don't wake up to feed as they should. These problems can be caused by prematurity, a lack of adequate nourishment from the mother's placenta, or drugs taken by the mother during pregnancy or labor. Some people think these babies are "good" because they demand so little, but the babies fail to get enough nourishment unless they are given extra coaxing.

Some babies may have painful physical problems that interfere with feeding. Muscle contractions in the neck and jaw, caused by birth trauma, can make latching on and sucking uncomfortable. Signs of jaw problems include clamping down and biting a lot, refusing to nurse on one side, and holding the head back or cocked to one side.

Some babies who are colicky and fuss at feeding time have a condition called *gastroesophageal* (or *gastrointestinal*) *reflux*, or GER. A lax sphincter between the esophagus and stomach causes these babies to frequently spit up or vomit significant volumes of milk. They may also suffer a painful burning sensation in the throat—that is, heartburn. In severe cases, babies may even develop ulcers deep in their throats. The symptoms of GER are crying and irritability at feeding time and soon after, and frequent waking at night, with wet patches of vomit under the baby's face. If the throat is very irritated, the vomit may contain small flecks of blood, resembling coffee grounds. About half of the babies diagnosed with GER have recurrent coughs, blocked wheezing, or periods when they stop breathing (*apnea*). Babies with severe GER tend to gain weight more slowly than normal.[59]

Gastroenterologists (sometimes called "GI specialists") deal with GER. They have special instruments for determining if a baby has it, including optical devices that allow them to look deep into the baby's throat. If the baby has GER, her esophagus will be swollen and red, and it may have red spots or ulcers on it. The doctor may recommend thickened formulas, keeping the baby upright in a seat after feeding, and medications to ease the baby's discomfort. Most babies outgrow GER between ten and eighteen months of age. In rare instances, GER may be caused by a hiatal hernia, a weakness or opening in the muscle that separates the chest from the abdomen, and this may require surgical correction.

If your baby is having trouble feeding, isn't gaining weight, or is losing weight, seek the help of a specialist right away. With good advice and patience, most babies' feeding problems can be overcome. Specialists who are skilled in helping babies with feeding disorders include lactation consultants (ask your doctor, midwife, or La Leche leader for the name of one in your area), physical and occupational therapists who specialize in working with babies (contact local chapters of United Cerebral Palsy or the Association for Retarded Citizens for a referral), and pediatric neurologists and specialists in failure-to-thrive syndrome (in teaching hospitals and medical schools).

CHAPTER FIVE

Train Yourself, Not Your Baby

IN THE EARLY MONTHS, most babies are very unpredictable. As you've probably already discovered, having a baby changes everything about your life. Old schedules and routines have to be thrown out the window because of that erratic little person who wakes you up at all hours of the night and may demand to nurse at any time and place.

Before the baby came, you got eight hours of sleep every night. Since the baby arrived, you are lucky to get two hours without interruption. Before the baby, you could post to-do lists on the refrigerator and be sure to check off every item. With the baby, you haven't enough time or energy to finish even a single item on the list.

Before the baby, you prided yourself on getting places on time, carrying out plans, and keeping to schedules. After the baby came, you put your watch in the dresser drawer, because you don't want to know that you are awake at 3:45 in the morning. Before the baby, you had grand schemes about your career and graduate school. With the baby, all you want out of life is a half hour to yourself to take a hot bath or to read the mail.

Typically, parents who have led very goal-oriented lives before the baby find the endless routines of parenthood daunting and very frustrating. They feel as though the baby is interfering with their basic rights to freedom of choice and movement. The simple tasks of packing a diaper bag, dressing the baby, finding the car keys, latching the baby in his car seat, putting the stroller in the trunk, and getting to the bank or grocery store loom as an overwhelming and exhausting challenge.

After a while the stress can precipitate a crisis. Your life as a parent isn't at all what you imagined. Parenthood doesn't seem to be all that it's cracked up to be. You may try to pretend that life can go on exactly as it did before the baby was born. You think the baby should adjust to *you*, and not the other way around.

This may be a familiar scene: You and your mate have just settled down to eat your first romantic little dinner together since the baby was born. The table is set. The meal is ready. The candles are lit. Your baby wakes up abruptly and starts screaming. Your milk lets down and leaks down the front of your blouse.

You and your partner desperately yearn to be together as you were when you courted, but now you've got a baby to care for. This may mean walking and rocking for hours. By the time the baby is back to sleep the food is cold, the candles have burned down, and the flicker of romance is gone.

Browsing in the childcare section of your bookstore, you come across a book whose cover announces "a revolutionary new approach to parenting your infant." The book proposes to teach babies how to calm themselves, "whether the problem is 'colic,' persistent crying and fussing, or sleep difficulties." Another book claims to "relieve most infants' persistent crying in three to seven days," while an even bolder cover declares that the text inside "can help you cure infant colic and soothe the crying within seven minutes." All of these books promise quick and easy answers to make your life "normal" again.

Because you're stressed and exhausted from the demands of your baby, these books and their promises seem very appealing, even seductive. You jump at the possibility that a writer may know some secret technique you haven't discovered to turn your baby into a placid, cooperative cherub.

Beware the Magic Cures

Books promising magic cures for normal infant crying and night waking are not all they pretend to be. In fact, by discouraging a parent's inborn responsiveness to a baby's needs, these books may actually do more harm than good.

To help you decide whether to use anyone's instant baby-training method, some explanation is needed about how these methods work. They are based on principles of animal training, especially on a concept called behavior modification.

"Parents these days often decide, 'Today she naps, tomorrow she doesn't.' What that says to me is that parents see the baby as an appendage hanging onto their lives. *'We'll put her down early if we want some time together. . . . We'll keep her up late if we want to take her to a movie with us.' Having a child is the greatest responsibility in the world. It's very, very wrong to pretend that life should go exactly as before."*

MAGDA GERBER
Cofounder, Resources for
Infant Educarers

Behavior modification, or "behavior mod," as it is popularly called, is best known by the work of B. F. Skinner, a psychologist who used feeding pellets to train nearly starved animals, like pigeons and rats, to do special tricks, such as turning around in a circle before being fed. Each time the animal got nearer to performing what the trainer wanted it to do, the animal would be rewarded with a food pellet, along with the shining of a light or the sounding of a buzzer. The animals learned quickly, and soon they would turn circles for the light or buzzer alone, as long as a pellet was dropped into the feeding tray every so often.

In time, specific principles emerged about how animals could be trained. Skinner discovered, for example, that giving animals rewards unpredictably worked far better than giving them predictably. If an animal was rewarded with a pellet and a flashing light every time it did the trick, the animal would quickly stop doing the trick if the trainer stopped giving the pellets. But if the trainer rewarded the animal with pellets randomly when the light flashed, the animal would keep doing the trick for either the light or the food indefinitely.

As the techniques for behavior modification have been developed and expanded through the years, they have been applied to human beings as well as animals. For example, profoundly retarded children have been taught to dress and toilet themselves through behavior modification, and children with severe emotional disorders have been helped to learn appropriate social behaviors. The most powerful behavior-shaping techniques use rewards (called "reinforcements"), such as candy or special favors, to induce the child to carry out the desired actions.

Researchers are now attempting to use behavior mod to train babies to act as their parents want them to act—that is, to cry less and sleep more. Unfortunately, some trainers, such as Dr. Richard Ferber, have developed methods that are punitive rather than rewarding to a baby. A baby's crying is self-punishing behavior. Ferber's method encourages parents to progressively ignore a baby's cries until the baby finally gives up and stops crying.

Other baby trainers manipulate babies in less punitive ways. They may tell parents to awaken the baby before he would awaken naturally, to teach the baby to soothe himself so he won't need them, or to use music or some other reward to keep the baby from crying or awakening them in the night.

A Comparison of Baby-Training Strategies

Source	Description	Baby's Age	Promised Outcome
Richard Ferber, M.D.: *Solve Your Child's Sleep Problems* (Simon & Schuster, 1985)	Parents are instructed to ignore their baby's crying for progressively longer periods of time— 5 minutes, 10 minutes, 15 minutes, up to 45 minutes after checking on the baby.	Varying age designations: "infant or toddler," 5 to 6 months old, 3 months old.	"Even an infant or toddler who has never slept through the night can be doing so within a few days with the right assistance from parents." "A young baby's sleep will show marked improvement, usually within a few days but at least within a week or two."
Bruce Taubman, M.D.: *Curing Infant Colic: The 7-Minute Program for Soothing the Fussy Baby* (Bantam Books, 1990).	After keeping a "behavior diary" on the baby for 24 hours, parents are referred to three flow charts of basic baby care strategies: holding/stopping holding, feeding/stopping feeding, waiting/picking up, giving pacifier, putting baby to bed, putting in infant seat and exposing to stimulation.	Not given; youngest baby in examples is 7 weeks old.	"You will be able to meet your baby's needs and stop the crying in seven minutes or less."
Ted Ayllon: *Stopping Baby's Colic: The New Program Designed to Relieve Most Infants' Persistent Crying in Three to Seven Days* (Perigee-Putnam, 1989)	"Comfort Training": Parents are instructed to reward their baby when he is quiet and alert with music—"classical, country and western, soft rock, jazz, show tunes or easy listening"—but to turn off the music when the baby cries.	"The youngest baby to be helped by this method was two weeks old and the oldest was five months."	"The inconsolable crying of the average baby can be controlled in three to seven days." "Your baby will go from being very restless and a 'pain' to be with to being peaceful and fun to be around."

Continued on next page

A COMPARISON OF BABY-TRAINING STRATEGIES—*Continued*

SOURCE	DESCRIPTION	BABY'S AGE	PROMISED OUTCOME
William H. Sammons, M.D.: *The Self-Calmed Baby: A Revolutionary New Approach to Parenting Your Infant* (Little, Brown and Company, 1989).	Recommends encouraging babies to calm themselves through sucking, positioning, moving, and looking at things. A 9-step process is suggested in approaching a crying baby: (1) talk to the baby from across the room, (2) go to the baby and rub his back, (3) roll the baby over and talk from a close range, (4) see if the baby will suck on his hand or your finger, (5) check his diaper, (6) pick up the baby and walk over to a chair, (7) talk to the baby again, (8) try letting the baby suck on his hand or your finger, (9) feed the baby.	No specific age range is given, although newborns are discussed.	Promises to make your child "sleep longer at night, nap at predictable times, travel better, feed more consistently, and be socially more responsive."
A variety of researchers*	"Scheduled Awakenings": Parents record babies' night wakings and crying episodes for a week. They then awaken the baby 15 to 30 minutes earlier than the baby would awaken on his own. The baby is supposed to gradually stop waking on his own. Parents awaken the baby less and less often until night waking has stopped completely.	Ages vary; 6 months to 2 1/2 years were the ages of babies in one study.	Some studies claim limited success. Researchers suggest that more investigation is needed.

*See: R. J. McGarr and M. F. Hovell, "In Search of the Sandman: Shaping an Infant to Sleep," *Education and Treatment of Children* 3 (1980): 173–82; C. M. Johnson, S. Bradley-Johnson, and J. M. Stack, "Decreasing the Frequency of Infants' Normal Crying with the Use of Scheduled Awakenings," *Family Practice Research Journal* I (1981): 98–104; C. M. Johnson and M. Lerner, "Effects of Scheduled Awakenings by Compliant Parents," *Infant Mental Health Journal* 6, no. 1 (1985): 21–30; and V. I. Rickert and C. M. Johnson, "Reducing Nocturnal Awakening and Crying Episodes in Infants and Young Children: A Comparison Between Scheduled Awakenings and Systematic Ignoring," *Pediatrics* 81, no. 2 (1988): 203–11.

Should You Override Your Baby's Signals?

The problem with most baby-training advocates is they have little understanding of the normal range of behavior for sleeping, waking, and crying among healthy babies. Research has demonstrated that individual babies vary just as much as adults do. Some babies sleep through the night from the first week onward, others not until they are four or five months old. Some sleep through the night during the early months and then begin to awaken again later, and some never sleep through the night during the first year.

Some babies seldom cry, whereas others may cry for hours each day. Some babies are mild-mannered, adaptable, and relatively easy to manipulate, whereas others are slow to adapt, intense in their responses, moody, and generally discontented. With the latter babies, attempts at training will probably not only fail, but make things worse.[60]

To convince parents to use their methods, baby-training advocates label normal infant waking and crying as unhealthy. Some, like Richard Ferber, resort to shaming techniques to convince parents they are doing wrong if they hesitate to follow the manipulative program. A parent's sin may be that he goes to his baby when the baby cries, or that she nurses her baby when the baby awakens hungry in the night.

You will spoil your baby, Ferber writes, if you "give in to every request, never say no, and abdicate your responsibility to decide for him what is best. . . . In the daytime it may be easier to distinguish your child's *wants* from his *needs*, and you will of course deny him any inappropriate requests without difficulty, even if he cries." Ferber admonishes that "a little extra crying—for a week or so—will not hurt him in the least."[61]

"Once your baby is about three months old, he or she no longer needs to be fed at bedtime and again several more times in the night," Ferber states flatly.[62] He warns breastfeeding mothers: "If you are breast feeding her and have to nurse more than one or two times during the night, you should also be suspicious that your child is getting too much milk, especially if each nursing lasts more than *two or three minutes*" (my emphasis). Ferber's program is designed to show you how to "help your child learn not to expect you and the nursing during the night."[63] Ferber fails to tell you that the tactics he proposes may also affect your milk supply, cause breast pain, and initiate weaning.

"My children never stopped crying after a reasonable amount of time. They never just whimpered and went back to sleep. They got more upset, until they worked themselves up to a pitch of hysteria."

"I've been told a thousand times to let them 'cry it out.' This never seemed right to me, no matter what age my child was. It never seemed fair to me that a dependent baby should be left to feel abandoned when he is incapable of understanding the reasons."

The thrilling claims of success reported by baby trainers have to be taken with a grain of salt. For one thing, these claims are seldom based on actual observations of babies; instead, they are based on parents' reports. Parents might sometimes fudge about how well the program is working, perhaps because they have "sinned" by comforting their babies in the night, or because they do not want themselves or their babies to appear to have failed.

When the claims to success are based on formal experiments, those experiments are likely to be seriously flawed. Most have involved only small numbers of babies over very short time spans. Usually, it is unclear whether the changes in sleeping or crying resulted from the training technique or the baby's maturation. Babies who aren't trained may stop waking up or crying anyway.[64]

In a number of the experiments in which babies have been left to cry, some of the babies have come down with colds or other illnesses, perhaps induced by stress. These babies have then been dropped from the study; only the babies who complete the training are figured in the results, which are therefore skewed.

The baby trainers offer little evidence that their methods are successful over the long term.[65] And some studies even indicate that a rebound effect may occur. Although a few babies may sleep longer or cry less for the duration of the study, they may begin waking again later, with greater frequency than ever before.

Finally, the training may do a baby long-term harm. Even if the techniques succeed in turning a demanding baby into a passive one, it is altogether possible that such passivity might indicate a more serious problem than crying or waking up in the night. It may signal that the baby has given up hope that his parents will respond to his cries for help. No reports demonstrate the effect the training may have on babies' behaviors and attitudes—especially their willingness to trust their parents and other people—one year, two years, or many years after.

The question whether to undertake training to keep your baby from crying or needing you in the night is an ethical one. Training your baby not to call upon you certainly isn't kind or compassionate. Your baby cannot talk, nor can he get to you if he is trapped in a crib. Crying is his only way of signaling you to help.

Can you in good conscience decide that you will respond to your baby's needs only when it is convenient for you, and only during daylight hours? At what point does the denial of a helpless infant's signals become child abuse and neglect?

Change Your *Behavior, Not Your Baby's*

Perhaps it's *you*, rather than your baby, who could use some training. After all, you can walk, talk, and decide for yourself about when you will eat or sleep, so a little change in the way you act won't hurt. To begin, you can use positive planning to help you cope with your baby's crying and waking without ignoring him or trying to keep him from calling for your help.

It's true that being solely responsible for the life of a tiny, dependent human being is very challenging. Your adaptive mechanisms are put to the most extreme test they may ever have to undergo. But this change in your lifestyle is not *bad*. Your job as a parent is to be present for your baby—to answer him, comfort him, and help him through. And this is an important and meaningful responsibility. Bringing a human being into the world, nurturing him, and rearing him is one of life's toughest jobs, but also potentially one of the most rewarding.

Simply put, you and your baby can adapt to each other more easily if you accept the baby and his demands as they are, rather than trying to make him be different than he is. Once you stop resisting a baby's demands and yield to them, life with the baby becomes more livable. Over and over, parents have told me about reaching a point of realization that, like it or not, the very special little person in their lives has special needs that must be met. Agreeing to meet those needs, rather than resisting them, brings parents into better harmony with their babies.

Your main job as a parent is to respond to your baby's cues. This means ignoring what your neighbor's baby is doing (sleeping through the night) or not doing (crying every night for two hours). Instead, consciously choose to accept your baby as a human being with real needs, who from birth onward can capably direct you in fulfilling those needs. A refreshing objectivity can now emerge. Instead of being eaten up with rage or guilt because your baby won't do what you think he should, you can simply accept that your baby is doing exactly what he should be doing.

"I think the most important thing for us was that we did what we knew we had to do, what our baby needed, not what friends or family thought was needed. We handled the comment that picking up will spoil the baby by saying: 'We, the family, are much happier when our baby is happy.' We had to be firm on that subject."

"Here's a statement I'd like to have engraved on stone: All healthy, normal infants do exactly what they can do and should be expected to do when they are ready. They should not be expected to do what they are not ready to do."

MAGDA GERBER

The inner logic goes something like this: "He's crying because he's uncomfortable." "He's sleeping because he needs rest." "He's asking me to carry him because it makes him feel better." "He wants to sleep next to me because he feels safer that way."

Regulating Your Life

Here is another way of adapting to parenthood, largely overlooked by most childcare manuals: Instead of waiting for the baby to become more predictable, or trying to force him into predictability, you make life more predictable for the baby. Just as you may expect to sit down to dinner at 6:00 P.M. every evening, babies like routine in their lives. The more daily routines you adopt, the easier things will be for both the baby and you, because your routines can help organize your baby's biological rhythms.[66]

I am not suggesting putting your baby on a feeding and sleeping schedule. You may have heard that a baby should be fed only once every four hours, or that he should be given only fifteen minutes at each breast, or that he should stay in his crib for a prescribed number of hours per night. Such prescriptions are based on a hypothetical "perfect baby," not on the needs of your unique child. Although offered with the surety of the Ten Commandments, these mandates for parenting are impractical, inhumane, and sometimes dangerous. When actually put into practice despite a baby's protests, schedules produce just what they're supposed to prevent—a clingy, insecure child.

The alternative to scheduling your baby is to gently work with him to create a predictable, daily sequence of activities. This means respecting his developing natural rhythms, not trying to change them radically. In time the baby's natural patterns will become better defined, and you can come to depend on them.

One technique many of the baby training experts use that *does* help is tracking a baby's sleeping and crying for several days to identify emerging patterns. You may find to your surprise that your baby's actions are not random, but rather predictable after all. Crying that seems to go on around the clock may be intense for only half an hour or so, at roughly the same time of day or night. You might discover that your baby is likely to sleep for several hours in the morning, to take a nap around the same time each afternoon, or to be fussy between 6:00 and 10:00 P.M.

When such patterns become clearer, you can begin to organize your life around your baby's needs. If your baby seems to be developing a pattern of taking his first nap in the morning between 8:00 and 10:00, then you don't dress him, throw him into the car, and go to the grocery store during that time. You may decide instead that you will prepare dinner and wash clothes when your baby sleeps in the morning, do errands at times when your baby is likely to be awake and amenable, or nap with the baby every afternoon.

If you can keep to a regular sequence of daily activities, your baby will begin to anticipate what comes next. Every morning when he first wakes up, for instance, you diaper him while leaning over to talk with him, and you present him with a small rattle to hold. Then you wrap him in a soft blanket, carry him to the rocker, feed and burp him, and then lay him down in his favorite sleeping position for a nap, if he seems to want to fall back to sleep. Or you put him in his infant seat and play with him, if he's wide awake and eager. Every afternoon you go for a walk with him in the carriage or baby pack. You put him down for his afternoon snooze on a quilt on the living room floor where the sun beams in.

Dad may have the urge to play vigorously with the baby when he gets home from work, but perhaps this seems to overstimulate the baby and make it hard for him to settle down to sleep. Instead, Dad can establish a soothing night routine that includes an outdoor walk followed by a warm bath, rocking, and humming a lullaby or turning on a music box.

"Babies give the people who care for them signals," says Mama Ruby Wright, a baby nurse for over twenty-five years.[67] If a baby is having trouble going to sleep, she tells parents, watch and listen carefully. Maybe he wants the booties off his feet, or the blanket off. Maybe he wants the blanket on his cheek, or his head against the crib bumper. Then again, maybe he's saying he can't stand anything touching his head or neck. Find out what he likes, and let him come to expect it.

To encourage the baby to sleep a longer stretch at night, Mama Ruby gently delays the last evening feeding. She sings to the baby, carries him around the room, and shows him things. She may play a music box, or hold the baby up to watch her face while she talks to him. She may tenderly exercise the baby's arms and legs, pat his back, or massage it. Minutes pass and the baby's hunger builds, but because he is intrigued, he barely complains. At last she checks the baby's diaper and changes it if it's wet. Fully tired and hungry, the baby nurses heartily, and then settles down for a stretch of uninterrupted sleep.

If your baby tends to be wakeful at night, it may help to expose him to the natural differences between daylight and nighttime darkness. Keeping a baby in a continuously lit nursery or bedroom can affect his sleeping patterns, so that he sleeps more in the daytime than at night. Make sure the bedroom is dark at night, and, during the day, let the baby nap in the sunshine. Swedish and Russian

---

TIPS FOR REGULATING YOUR BABY'S LIFE—AND YOUR OWN

✔ Postpone long trips until your baby's sleeping and waking patterns become more regular.

✔ Keep errands to a minimum, and do them the same time each day.

✔ Make the difference between awake time and sleep time obvious. In the daytime have the baby nap in a light, airy, somewhat noisy room, or outdoors.

✔ Take your baby outside for at least a half hour each day, and about the same time each day. The sunshine is good for the baby, and it may help him move toward more daytime wakefulness and nighttime sleepiness.

✔ Change the baby's diaper before daytime feedings so that he awakens fully.

✔ If bathing invigorates your baby, bathe him during the day instead of the evening.

✔ At night, turn the television or stereo down or off. Keep lights dim.

✔ Make your baby's nighttime sleep place a quiet zone, with few toys, mobiles, and other distractions.

✔ Avoid stimulating the baby at night with eye-to-eye contact, caresses, play, or talk.

✔ Stay in the bedroom when the baby awakens at night. Keep the room dark, or use a nightlight.

✔ Use double diapers and waterproof pants, or disposables, to avoid nighttime diaper changes.

---

mothers have their babies nap outdoors even in the middle of winter. Their babies are swaddled soundly, with only their faces exposed, and placed outside in their carriages. Not only is the fresh air healthful, but the exposure to daylight helps turn the babies' inner clocks toward night sleeping.

Feeding a baby more in the daytime may help reduce the number of night feedings. Letting your baby nap in the sunshine—within hearing of singing birds and playing children—will probably keep his naps short. But if your baby is a heavy sleeper, you might try awakening him from naps to offer a feeding. Nursing him every hour or two (or bottle-feeding him every two and a half to three hours) during the day may help him sleep longer at night. (Be aware, though, that some babies become more fussy, sleepless, and liable to spit up or vomit when they are overfed.)

Besides working with your baby's developing patterns, you may want to brainstorm about possible changes in your family's lifestyle that would make it easier for you to care for your baby. Could your partner take over the dishwashing or laundry? Could you and the baby both benefit from more fresh air? Might your older children also enjoy a daily walk, and adapt well to a "quiet time" during the baby's nap? How can you get more support from your relatives or friends? For practical suggestions, see chapter 10, "Taking Care of Yourself," and "Resources for Parents," pages 153–55.

"My baby slept a little and cried a lot. Even as a newborn she slept only a half an hour at a time, and when she was awake, she cried if she wasn't nursing. In time things were much better. By the time she reached six months of age she began to improve. Now at age four she is making up for lost time; she sleeps nine to ten hours at night, plus she still takes a two hour nap every afternoon."

CHAPTER SIX

Does Your Baby Have Colic?

JENNIFER HOLLOWAY is a beautiful, rosy cheeked, blue-eyed two-month-old. When she's out shopping with her parents, people often stop to tell her parents how adorable she is. Back home, though, Jennifer isn't so adorable. She seems to cry constantly. She often refuses to look her mother and father in the eyes. She acts like she wants to squirm right out of their arms. Yet when they try to put her down she cries even more inconsolably. Jennifer is usually calm when her mother carries her in a front pack—as long as her mother doesn't stop walking. Even diaper changing provokes loud screams of protest.

A few gulps into her feeding and Jennifer starts fussing. Within moments, she's screaming. Her cries are so loud and shrill her parents can barely endure them. Her cycles of discomfort and screaming go on day and night, broken only by brief rests. Her parents have started to worry about getting evicted from their apartment because of the noise.

Unless she is being carried, Jennifer rarely naps for more than a half hour. She won't go to sleep at night until her parents do, and then she awakens every hour or two. When bedtime nears, the prospect of another night of continually interrupted sleep fills her parents with dread, as their bodies cry out for much-needed rest.

Sometimes parents and nurses know within hours after a birth that they've got a very fussy infant on their hands. Such a baby may be somewhat soothed in her family's constant care, but the impersonal routines of a hospital may be intolerable to her. A "screamer" may have her bassinet set off in a far corner of the nursery so that her unending cries don't upset other babies.

Here's how one nurse described the behavior of a baby boy in her daily progress notes:

> Babies never annoy me but this one does. I've never seen a baby act like this before. It seems that nothing satisfies him but holding him. It was suggested that I'd just have to hold him in one arm and work with the other until he falls asleep. The baby seemed miserable and uncomfortable. He sputtered and whimpered. In 20 minutes he burst forth again full force. Picked up and patted, almost lulled to sleep, he was replaced in the crib. He went to sleep, was quiet but woke up shortly and suddenly started crying again. Dropped off to sleep and again awoke crying, off and on until midnight. Finally he went to sleep and slept for three and a half hours.[68]

Not all babies are as difficult to manage as this newborn and Jennifer, but many have frequent periods of intense crying that appear to be pain-related. Some cry night and day. Others cry mostly in the evenings, and still others are unpredictable about when they cry. When a baby cries frequently and inconsolably and her complaint seems unexplainable, she is usually said to have colic.

What Is Colic?

It has been estimated that over seven hundred thousand U.S. babies each year suffer from colic.[69] A colicky baby, according to physicians and researchers, is one "who is otherwise healthy and well fed, has paroxysms of irritability, fussing or crying lasting for a total of more than three hours a day and occurring on more than three days in any one week."[70] The long crying bouts typically begin within a few weeks of birth and last about three months, which is why the English call the condition "three-month colic." Sometimes, however, colicky behavior continues for six months or more.

Colic occurs with equal frequency among boy and girl babies, and first-born and subsequent children. Although colic is unknown in some societies in which babies are constantly carried, it occurs regardless of racial heritage. And the condition is by no means unique to bottle-fed babies. Forty-three percent of the breastfeeding mothers in a British survey reported that their babies four weeks of age and under had colic. Thirty-nine percent of the mothers who had switched from breastfeeding to artificial feeding by four weeks

"One night at three A.M., when the baby had been crying steadily for four hours and would not stop, when we were worried that she might be really ill, when we were afraid our whole apartment building could hear and would be down the next morning demanding that we move out immediately, we sat down on our living room sofa and cried together. All three of us."

"If you're wondering if your baby has colic—he doesn't. With a colicky baby, there's no doubt!"

reported colic, as did 44 percent whose babies were receiving both breast milk and artificial milk.[71]

Almost eighty years ago, Dr. Emelyn Coolidge described a typical colic attack in the same way that all major pediatric textbooks do today:

> The baby with colic screams lustily and in paroxysms. His face is first red, but it may become pale or even blue around the mouth if the attacks last long or are severe. The hands and feet are cold, the legs are drawn up, the abdomen, as a rule, is very hard and distended, and the baby works his hands in agony.[72]

Parents concur with this description. Recently Dr. Michael Woolridge and his associates at the University of Bristol in England asked 1,160 English mothers to define colic and to tell if their babies had it. The mothers agreed about the main symptom of colic—crying and more crying. Seventy-eight percent identified continuous or consistent crying or screaming, spasmodic crying, or crying for which the baby couldn't be comforted. Seventy-five percent said that the colicky baby draws up her legs, clenches her fists, screws up her face, and winces as she cries. During a colic attack, many mothers said, a baby's cries are markedly more intense than at other times, and easy to distinguish from normal hunger cries. Thirty-four percent identified abdominal pain or stomach cramps as colic symptoms, and only 18 percent identified the buildup of severe gas in the baby's gut. Few mothers found colic attacks to cluster around 6:00 to 9:00 P.M., as they are often said to do.[73]

What Causes Colic?

Doctors and scientists have been trying to find the cause of colic for over half a century now. The reports from hundreds of studies of colicky babies are confusing and often contradictory. Some have claimed miracle cures that are hard to believe—babies suddenly got better when parents kept their booties on twenty-four hours a day, or fed them sugar water, or took eyelashes out of their eyes. Most of these studies involved only a few colicky babies and no controls, so we can't know whether the cure really worked or whether the babies got better because they outgrew the problem or their diet or environment changed. More often than not, the results of these studies could not be duplicated when the experiments were run again.

Perhaps the most valuable colic studies have focused on the baby's belly. Throughout history, people have believed that the constantly crying baby was experiencing some kind of abdominal pain; the word *colic*, in fact, comes from the Greek work *kolikos*, an adjective derived from *kolon*, meaning the large intestine. We still don't know, however, whether belly pain is always or even usually the cause of crying in the many babies said to suffer from colic. Some parents assume their babies have bellyaches because they draw up their legs when they cry, but babies do this when they hurt in any part of the body. Besides, specialists believe babies can't localize pain—that is, no matter where the hurt originates, babies feel it in the abdominal region. Still, when you can hear your baby's belly gurgling, and when she doesn't calm down until you lay her on your arm and massage her abdomen, you *know* your baby's crying has to do with her digestion.

IMMATURE DIGESTIVE SYSTEM. Compared with most other young mammals, a human baby is born in an extremely immature state. Like a kangaroo infant, who rides in its mother's pouch, or an opossum infant, who latches on to its mother's tail, human babies are neurologically incomplete.

A baby's digestive system, particularly the lower part, is especially slow to mature. At one month of age, a baby's stomach capacity is only one-tenth that of an adult. The baby's digestive tract contains few digestive enzymes, important agents for breaking down food substances. Gastric glands in the stomach, which secrete digestive acids, are also remarkably sparse in a baby—4 percent as numerous as in an adult. Muscle layers surrounding the baby's stomach and intestines are relatively thin and weak. The baby's intestines are substantially shorter than a child's or an adult's, and they lack the ridges and tiny, hairlike filaments that help in the processing of food and waste in an older person's body. The graceful squeezings and releasings of peristalsis are faint or totally absent in a newborn's intestines; instead, food is propelled by sudden spasms. Because of a lack of muscular tone in the sphincter between the stomach and esophagus, milk may move upward from the stomach and out the baby's mouth. For all these reasons, digestion can be an uncomfortable process for a baby. And it may take months before a baby's digestive system begins to function smoothly and painlessly.

RESEARCH ON BELLYACHES. Digesting food seems more difficult for some babies than for others. In 1952, a Swedish researcher named Sigvard Jorup found that the colons of colicky babies contracted violently during feedings, propelling the entire contents quickly forward. Whereas a baby's colon normally takes several hours to empty, in these babies the colon emptied in as little as half a minute, X-rays showed. The contractions began the moment food rounded the S-shaped curve at the end of the colon, just before it empties into the rectum. At this precise moment a baby would raise her legs toward her belly and abruptly stop nursing to cry. When the colon contractions ceased, the baby would relax and resume nursing—*unless* the muscles stayed contracted, as they did in some babies. In these cases, the babies fussed through the entire feedings. Jorup found that the colicky babies averaged five bowel movements a day, whereas normal breastfed babies had only one to three.[74]

Colicky babies may have imbalances among the hormones that control intestinal contraction and relaxation. Some studies have shown that these babies have lower levels of progesterone, a hormone that helps to relax the muscles of the intestines. At birth a baby usually has a high level of progesterone, but the supply runs out within a week or two, and the baby must begin to produce her own—at just about the time that colic attacks typically start. In one study colicky babies got better after being given extra progesterone.[75] The long-term effects of administering such a powerful hormone to fussy babies are not yet known, however.

Another researcher has found that colicky babies have higher levels of motilin, a digestive hormone that stimulates muscle contractions in the baby's gut. In colicky babies, motilin levels were high from birth onward, although colic symptoms didn't show up until later.[76]

AILMENTS THAT MASK AS COLIC. By paying attention to symptoms other than crying, parents can often identify specific ailments that cause bellyaches and fussing.

Some babies, especially those who are formula-fed, get constipated. Going even a day without a bowel movement can make a baby quite fussy, if she normally has a stool more often. She may grunt and cry, and demand to nurse frequently but stop soon after starting. Infant-size glycerin suppositories can help with occasional constipation, although using them frequently may make a baby dependent on them. Abdominal massage can also help to produce a bowel movement (see page 26).

If your baby has been constipated since birth, or if she is chronically constipated, you should consult a doctor. Your baby may have a too-tight anus, or even an obstruction in the digestive tract. If she is bottle-fed, she may need a dietary change; if she is breastfed and under a month old, you'll want to make sure she is getting enough milk (breastfed babies are seldom truly constipated). A constipated baby may have an anal fissure—a sore on the anus that makes bowel movements painful, adding to a baby's complaints.

Sometimes babies said to be colicky are reacting to something in their mother's diet or in their formula. Allergic babies usually have symptoms besides abdominal pain, such as diarrhea, greenish or frothy stools, rashes, frequent spitting up or vomiting, and gassiness. Gas-producing fruits and vegetables can make a baby as well as her mother feel bloated and pass a lot of gas. (See chapter 7, "The Colic-Allergy Connection.")

Bellyaches and crying may also be caused by an imbalance in a baby's foremilk and hindmilk intake. In such a case the baby typically gains weight faster than average but spits up a lot. Letting a baby nurse to her satisfaction on one side before switching to the other usually solves the problem.

A baby who spits up a lot, vomits, and fusses at feeding time may have a condition called gastroesophageal reflux—that is, excessive regurgitation. Babies usually outgrow this condition, but serious cases need treatment (see page 59).

Thrush, a yeast infection in the mouth and digestive tract, can make a baby fussy, gassy, and reluctant to nurse (see page 99).

CONDITIONS DURING PREGNANCY AND BIRTH. For some babies, crying and irregular sleep-wake cycles are a prolonged physical reaction to events that occurred before they were born. Babies who have been born prematurely or much smaller than average, or who have suffered oxygen deprivation and birth complications, are more likely to cry a lot than babies who haven't had these experiences. They are also more likely to have irregular sleep-wake cycles.

Babies whose mothers have had high blood pressure during pregnancy are more likely to be overexcitable and fussy than those whose mothers have had normal blood pressure.[77]

The use of epidural anesthesia in labor may be related to a baby's later colicky behavior. Australian researchers compared forty babies of mothers who had epidurals with forty babies born without drugs. By the fifth day after birth, babies in the epidural group cried more frequently than the babies of unmedicated mothers. When the babies were one month old, those of medicated mothers were less adaptable, more intense, and far more difficult to manage than the babies of the undrugged mothers.[78]

Babies of mothers who took drugs in pregnancy often have nervous system instabilities. They are likely to be extremely fussy and have sleep disruptions if their mothers have used a lot of heroin, smoked a lot of marijuana, or drunk heavily while pregnant. Babies born to mothers who have taken barbiturates during pregnancy are more liable to be overexcitable, trembling, restless, and ravenous. Their symptoms may not appear until a week after birth. They usually peak between two and six weeks, but some symptoms linger until the baby is about six months old. Babies whose mothers have used cocaine in pregnancy are likely to be jittery and hyperactive, to scream shrilly, and to have feeding problems and irregular sleep-wake cycles. They are also likely to show signs of central nervous system immaturity, such as very tight or very limp muscles.[79]

Babies whose mothers have smoked tobacco during pregnancy, or who live in households where there is heavy smoking, are more likely than other babies to be irritable and agitated, particularly after feedings. A French study found that 91 percent of the babies with two smoking parents were fussy after feedings, and 57 percent of babies whose mothers alone smoked were fussy.[80]

The Colicky Temperament

In his study of colicky babies and their spastic colons, Sigvard Jorup found these babies also shared a distinctive sort of temperament. "They are, in general, impatient and irritable," he noted. "They have difficulty in relaxing, are wakened on the least occasion, become fretful and impatient, and take a long time to calm down again. They twist and turn, kick, and display motor restlessness in general. Their sleep is shorter and less sound than that of normal babies."[81]

One characteristic of these babies, Jorup found, was extreme sensitivity to noises or light. The click of an X-ray machine would make them startle. The sound of a voice or the scraping of a chair, a creaking door or approaching footsteps, would make these babies awaken and cry. Their mothers noticed that they would awaken and scream if an overhead light was turned on, and they couldn't sleep at all if a light was left on in the room.

In the years since Jorup's study, certain phrases have turned up over and over in reports on colicky babies—*delicate, highly nervous, over-ready response to stimulation, overreactive,* and *tense.* One researcher described these babies as having a "lean and hungry look" about them. They seem to want the world to go away, because they are unable to deal with all of its sights and sounds. They don't want to be carried or jiggled—they become unglued from too much motion.

They seem acutely aware of sensations inside their bodies, too, such as intestinal spasms or the pressure of an air bubble in the stomach. It's as though their ability to screen out or dampen these sensations still needs time to develop.

"In many cases the colicky baby has an abnormally low threshold for organic stimulation. The baby is attuned to body processes that most babies are able to ignore," notes Alan Lake, a pediatric gastroenterologist at the Johns Hopkins University School of Medicine. The reason for a baby's lowered awareness threshold is not clearly understood, but Dr. Lake believes it may be connected to an immature nervous system.[82] Many researchers, in fact, think that a disorganized, overtaxed central nervous system is the basic cause of colic.

Many fussy babies seem to need *extra* stimulation to keep from crying. They want their parents to do *anything* to take their minds off their discomfort—to rock, to walk, to sing, or to talk to them. If nothing exciting is happening they want to nurse continuously. This type of baby might quiet down only if you walk her up and down the stairs, jiggling her continuously, at 2:00 A.M. Such stimulation apparently overrides pain, at least temporarily.

THE NERVOUS-MOTHER MYTH. On the verge of tears, you confess to the pediatrician that your baby is crying day and night. After a routine physical exam, the doctor announces, "There's nothing physically wrong with your baby that I can see. She seems to be gaining weight and thriving. She probably just has colic."

Then he glances at you in an appraising way and adds, "You seem a little tense. Try to relax, and she'll probably settle right down." Then he rushes off to see the next little patient.

You feel like screaming, "You'd be tense, too, if you had to deal with a baby like mine!" But you keep silent. Your baby's pediatrician seems to be confirming your deepest fear—there's something wrong with *you* that's causing your baby's suffering.

That a mother's nervousness causes her baby's colic is an old notion, one that is often revived when a doctor can't find a physical reason for a baby's distress. Psychologists have even conducted tests to show a correlation between a baby's fussiness and her parents' nervousness. The tests could not explain, however, how Baby Number One and Baby Number Two in a family could turn out even-tempered, whereas Baby Number Three is a screamer. Did the baby's mother or father suddenly change temperaments? How is it that anxious parents can give birth to easy babies, whereas some very relaxed parents have difficult babies?

"I've come to the conclusion that a colicky baby is usually a very sensitive one. Our baby always seemed more sensitive to strangers, to noise, and so forth, than her peers. Now she is a sensitive toddler, very alert and curious and bright."

"My husband and I would like to have another child, but we both still shudder at the idea of having to go through another experience of colic like our baby's. It was truly a nightmare. Only parents who have gone through colic like we have can really understand."

Of course, parents of colicky babies often *are* more tense than mothers of calm, easy babies with regular sleeping patterns. This is because caring for a sleepless, constantly crying baby is very stressful. Ronald Illingworth, a British pediatrician and colic researcher, believes parents aren't to blame for their babies' colic:

> In my opinion, most of the so-called tension in parents of babies with colic is the result of the babies' colic and not the cause of it. . . . After careful observation of parents of these babies, I do not believe that they are any different from parents of babies who have no colic. . . . I do not see how family tension could produce these strictly rhythmical attacks of violent screaming . . . which should surely be due to pain [judging] from the nature of the scream[s] and the fact that they continue unabated in the mother's arms. If the colic was due entirely to psychological tension, one would expect it to occur more often in the first-born than in subsequent children, but it does not. Furthermore, colic commonly occurs in only one of three or four babies in the family.[83]

Perhaps the reason colic studies have been so inconclusive is that the concept of colic is so vague. Having colic is like having a headache. Your head may hurt in the back, at the temples, around the eyes, in the sinuses, or all over, yet you simply say you have a headache. A lot of things cause headaches—allergies, hunger, anemia, and so on—and various causes may be interrelated. We can't pinpoint a single cause of headaches, nor can we identify one for colic.

Colic is even more mysterious than headaches, because babies can't talk. They can't tell us where they hurt, or how badly they hurt. All they can do is cry. In applying the label *colic* we are describing not what babies feel, but what we hear—intense crying.

In the future, researchers may come to understand colic better. They may be able to isolate a bacteria or virus, a gene, or a nutritional deficiency that causes babies to cry inconsolably. Perhaps they'll discover why babies are more liable to cry at mealtimes, or why they draw up their legs when they scream. But chances are they'll never find a *single* cause of colicky pain and distress.

Some of the conditions commonly labeled colic can be identified and treated; food sensitivities, for instance, may be managed by dietary changes. But if temperament or immaturity is the only identifiable cause of a baby's misery, only patient nurturing can help. Remedies for colic often only mask the symptoms, and many are dangerous.

Folk Remedies for Colic

Although their effectiveness has rarely been scientifically tested, many popular colic remedies have been in use for generations. Some mothers say a teaspoon of warm water before a feeding relaxes a baby's digestive system. Others use an infusion of fennel or anise seeds; a tablespoonful of seeds are boiled in a cup of water, and the seeds are strained out. Chamomile tea has been traditionally used for calming nervous persons of all ages, but it can cause a reaction in those who are allergic to ragweed, its close relative. Peppermint tea and dill water, made from dillweed, have also been given to colicky babies, as have bay leaf tea and gum arabic (one drop to a teaspoon of warm formula or breast milk). Some parents recommend Hylands Homeopathic Colic Tablets, available in health food stores and some drugstores, and others swear by ginger ale.

Alcohol has been a popular colic remedy for centuries. It was once given to babies in a "sugar tit," a handkerchief wrapped around a lump of sugar and dipped in liquor. Gripe water, alcohol mixed with dill syrup, is still widely sold in England and Canada. And some physicians still casually recommend giving a fussy baby whiskey. But beware: Alcohol is a dangerous drug for babies, so dangerous that it is listed in poison control centers across the nation. A baby's body does not react to alcohol in the same way that an adult's does. Even small amounts can cause severe hypoglycemia, or low blood sugar. This can result in profuse sweating, tremors, and possibly coma.

Opium was once also a common remedy for colic. In the nineteenth century it was used in "soothing syrups" and teething powders. Paregoric, camphorated tincture of opium, is still sometimes prescribed for colicky babies. Besides being sleep-inducing, opium is habit-forming.

Although many doctors have criticized mothers for doping their babies with alcohol and opium, the drugs doctors prescribe for fussy babies are often just as dangerous, or more so. (Be sure to read chapter 9, "Doctors, Disease, and Drugs.") Alcohol, opium, tranquilizers, and other drugs may stop a baby's crying, but they generally do not affect the cause of the baby's distress. Parents should be very cautious about giving a baby *any* drug.

"It must be my fault. I must be the most horrible person in the world because of what I'm feeling right now."

"It seems to me a big part of dealing with a fussy baby, or a whining two-year-old, is dealing with one's own needs and expectations. Everything interlocks so. We had feelings of anger and bitterness toward our colicky baby. Looking back now, I know they were normal feelings, but at the time I didn't know that. Even people with normal babies get frustrated and angry. How can you help it, listening to a screaming child all day and night while you're worn to a frazzle?"

Coping with Colic

It's only natural to judge your success as a parent by your baby's reactions to you. Having a placid, contented cherub helps a parent feel competent and self-assured, but a colicky baby who looks up at you with a contorted, angry face and bombards you with piercing screams day and night is bound to make you feel as if you've failed somehow.

Shattered expectations are hard to face. During pregnancy you probably cherished fantasies about your coming baby. Romantic expectation is one way people mentally prepare themselves for an upcoming life change. It happens when teenagers dream about careers and when lovers dream about marriage. Your dreams about your baby during pregnancy helped you to pave the way for the commitment and work your baby would soon require of you.

It is a crushing blow to wake up to the fact that you didn't give birth to the smiling Ivory Snow baby you dreamed about. Instead you created a tiny, screaming monster who appears to be taking over every moment of your life. "If I could just feel more *positive* about being a parent," you reason with yourself, "then maybe everything would get better."

Many parents go through cycles of wondering what they've done to make their babies act the way they do. A typical inner dialogue might sound like this: "Maybe I shouldn't have had wine with dinner when I was pregnant. Maybe it was the epidural I had. Maybe I didn't take enough childbirth education classes. Maybe my breasts aren't making enough milk. Maybe the baby knows I'm a klutz, and she's mad at me because I don't know what I'm doing."

It's a rare parent who doesn't feel violated when her baby fails to match deeply cherished dreams.[84] When people's dreams are shattered, they first try to pretend that everything is all right; then they may begin to feel really angry or depressed. For suggestions about dealing with your feelings see chapter 10, "Taking Care of Yourself," and chapter 11, "Overcoming Stress and Depression."

The Danger of Turning Off

Parent-baby relationships are reciprocal in nature. Babies react to their parents' personalities, and parents react to their babies'. A lovable, easygoing baby may be able to warm up even the most insecure and aloof caregiver. And a very difficult, miserable baby may turn off even the most experienced and eager parents.

One of the problems of having a colicky baby is that she makes you less eager to interact with her. It's not her fault; she really can't help how she feels or how she acts. But if she's not rewarding to be with, you may actually begin to avoid her, anticipating that you'll only be stressed and frustrated if you try to engage with her.

Dr. Susan Goodman Campbell, of the University of Pittsburgh, has studied babies who were rated by their mothers as "extremely irregular, nonadaptable, and negative in mood." She found that the mothers of these infants spent significantly less time interacting with their babies than did mothers who judged their babies as easier. The mothers of difficult babies talked less to the babies, and responded less to their crying and willingness to play. When the difficult babies reached eight months old, their mothers were ignoring them even more than they had earlier.[85]

It doesn't help to compare your baby with someone else's and then to draw conclusions about your baby, or about your parenting abilities, based on that comparison. Judge your baby as "bad," and she may stay that way; judge yourself as "bad," and you may end up a bad parent. You and your baby both have strengths that can't be measured by imagining what things are like next door. If you are bugged by your neighbor's gushing about her placid baby, perhaps you should seek out other parents of colicky babies.

Parents who understand what you are going through, as well as sympathetic family members, can help you in coping with a fussy, extra-needy baby. Support from others can protect you from feeling isolated and helpless; it can strengthen you against all the stress you're undergoing. Finding support can ensure that you don't turn off to your baby, even though he may not give you much encouragement. (See "Resources for Parents," pages 153–55.)

Will She Always Be Like This?

Many babies outgrow colic at about three months of age, making their parents feel as if they've suddenly acquired a new, much happier baby. Other babies continue to fuss through the first six months or longer. Parents report that even babies who are extra-demanding throughout infancy often become more manageable around four months of age.

"Inside I felt miserable and disillusioned with motherhood. I was caught in the dreadful trap of comparing myself with other women. Instead of wondering what I was doing wrong that my baby wasn't a sleeping, smiling cherub, I needed to accept the fact that he wasn't and to praise my mothering skills despite their seeming ineffectiveness."

"Now, at two years, our formerly colicky son is a very loving, secure child. I believe the extra care and concern shown during his difficult time has carried over and helped him to be secure and giving. The time we spent with him trying to keep him from fussing has really given him a boost in language and intellectual development."

Babies' personality traits seem to be transient. In fact, a child's temperament often makes a complete turnabout between infancy and the preschool years. A quiet, introspective preschooler is more likely to have been a highly intense baby than a "good" one.[86]

In a study that followed babies from the age of four months to seven years, three-fourths of the babies considered difficult by their parents acquired calmer temperaments later on. And 61 percent of the easygoing babies were later labeled difficult![87]

CHAPTER SEVEN

The Colic-Allergy Connection

COLICKY CRYING AND FUSSINESS can be caused by a baby's difficulty in processing substances in his diet, or even in the air. The baby may have an allergic reaction—that is, his immune system may mobilize against the substance—or he may have one of various other physical reactions. In the latter case he is considered "hypersensitive."

Food Intolerances

Food allergies and hypersensitivities can occur among breastfed as well as bottle-fed babies. Very small particles of allergenic food substances—smaller than can be detected by a microscope—can pass through breast milk to a baby.

Some babies become sensitized to certain food substances while they are still in the womb. Egg antigens—microscopic fighters against egg proteins—have been found in the fluid of infants' amniotic sacs, in the blood of their umbilical cords, and in their dark, sticky meconium stools right after birth. Receiving egg protein through their mothers' milk, or eating eggs later, may spark a strong allergic reaction in those babies born with allergic sensitivities.

SYMPTOMS OF REACTION. Most young babies can't absorb all the lactose (milk sugar) in formulas. Breastfed babies have the same problem when they take in too much foremilk in relation to hindmilk, usually because they're switched from one breast to the other before they have sucked to satisfaction at the first (see page 48). When lactose isn't fully digested it ferments in the lower intestine, producing excessive acid and gas. About 15 percent of the gas gets absorbed into the baby's bloodstream; the rest is passed as gas. The acids are either absorbed into the mucous lining of the baby's colon, or they stay in the lower intestinal tract, causing painful cramping and diarrhea.

Certain starches, such as those in baby cereals, can set off a similar chain of reactions in a baby's gut. This is because young babies have only about one-tenth the starch-digesting capacity of adults. One study found colic to be more prevalent in a group of babies fed cereal in the first three months than in a group who were given no solids.[88] Some people believe that feeding solids—by mixing cereal into formula or starting a baby on puréed foods—helps the baby to sleep through the night, but this has proven false.[89]

Babies with true allergies may also have intestinal cramps and fuss a lot, but they typically have other symptoms as well. They may spit up a lot or vomit occasionally, and they may have frothy or greenish stools or diarrhea, possibly with blood in the stool. They may also have rashes, stuffy or drippy noses, and wheezing. In rare cases a baby may react to an allergen so strongly that he goes into shock, his airway is obstructed, and he must be rushed to the hospital.

Allergies can also affect a baby's sleep. When eight bottle-fed babies who had been waking over and over in the night were given a special formula with altered milk protein instead of a standard cow's milk-based formula, their sleep patterns became more normal. When the standard formula was reintroduced into the babies' diets, they again developed sleeplessness. Tests showed that the babies were having allergic reactions. Among the babies' other symptoms were wheezing and eczema.[90]

Allergies can affect a child's health in less direct ways as well. They can cause swollen tonsils, congested sinuses, swollen mucous membranes in the Eustachian tube, and fluid in the middle ear. These conditions can lead to chronic inflammation of the middle ear, which in turn can make the baby prone to chronic bacterial infections of the ear. Children who have allergies, or family histories of allergies, are thus more likely to develop ear infections than nonallergic children.[91] Allergic children may be more prone to other infections as well. When white blood cells are tied up fighting food residues, fewer may be available to attack disease organisms.[92]

CAUSES OF FOOD ALLERGIES. Feeding a baby solids too early can provoke later allergic reactions. Children who have been given solids before the age of six months are more likely to develop allergies than those who have been solely breastfed.

Formula feeding, too, carries the risk of setting off allergic reactions. Soy-based formulas as well as cow's milk-based formulas can cause these reactions, because the proteins and sugars in soy-based formulas have allergenic qualities similar to those in cow's milk. Twenty-five percent of infants with milk allergy develop an allergy to soy, says Dr. William Crook.[93] For this reason, the American Academy of Pediatrics has issued a formal statement recommending that soy-based formulas not be used as a replacement for cow's milk-based formulas when a baby is known to be allergic to cow's milk protein, or as a way of managing colic. Special formulas with altered milk proteins and sugars, called hydrolysate formulas (such as Progestimil or Nutramigen), are considered a better choice, though they are costly.[94]

A baby's allergic tendency may be inherited. Babies whose grandparents, mothers, fathers, or siblings have eczema, asthma, hay fever, or other allergies are more likely to have allergic reactions than babies whose family members don't have any of these conditions.[95]

Babies who have been given antibiotics may also be at a higher risk for developing food allergies. Antibiotics have been linked to the "leaky gut syndrome," in which the intestinal lining becomes first inflamed, then thin and porous. Incompletely digested proteins are absorbed intact through the intestine to the bloodstream, where white blood cells attack them as if they were foreign invaders.[96]

Some doctors think the increasing incidence of food allergies is due to overconsumption of particular foods. If you are breastfeeding, an unvaried diet, especially if it is composed mainly of refined foods, may lead to the development of food intolerances in your baby.

COMMON ALLERGENIC FOODS. More babies are allergic to cow's milk than to any other food. Some are allergic to proteins in the milk. Researchers have recently discovered that most breastfeeding mothers also transmit cow antibodies through their milk, and that mothers whose milk has high levels of these antibodies are more likely to have colicky babies.[97]

Breastfed babies can react to other foods in a mother's diet besides milk. Chocolate, which contains a caffeine-like substance called theobromine, can cause irritability, diarrhea, and vomiting in a baby.

"My breastfed baby had colic, and I found that sometimes things I ate consistently caused gas pain at certain times of day, depending on when I ate them. Eggs were one of the worst. I gave them up, and it made a big difference. I had to avoid even things that had eggs in them. It was like getting a different baby. It took about two days to see the change, and it can take longer."

Citrus and other acidic fruits (tomatoes, pineapples, strawberries) often cause reactions, most commonly when a mother drinks large quantities of juice. Eggs are another common allergen.

Less common allergens are wheat and corn (including all foods made with corn syrup) and soy proteins, which are in many processed foods besides formula, tofu, and soy sauce. Nuts and, especially, peanuts can be allergenic, and so can fish and shellfish.

Your baby may be hypersensitive to other substances in your diet. The caffeine in coffee, tea, or cola can make a baby irritable and jittery. Cyclamates (artificial sweeteners) taken in large quantity by a breastfeeding mother can cause vomiting and diarrhea in her baby. Senna, included in some herbal tea blends, can also give a baby diarrhea. Gas-producing vegetables, such as beans, cabbage, and onions, can cause flatulence in a breastfed baby as well as his mother. Nicotine is detectable in the milk of mothers who smoke as few as one cigarette a day. It can make a baby fussy, while the smoke can contribute to respiratory and ear infections.

A baby may be hypersensitive to certain dietary supplements, whether they are given to him directly or taken by his breastfeeding mother. Some babies react to iron in their formula and feel better when they're given an iron-free version. Others become less irritable when synthetically colored or flavored vitamin drops are stopped. Fluoride, in vitamins given to a breastfeeding mother or her baby, can cause rashes and gastrointestinal upsets in the baby. Brewer's yeast, which some mothers take as a source of B-complex vitamins, can also cause gastric distress in a breastfed baby.

PREVENTING FOOD ALLERGIES. If you have allergies, or if they run in your family or your spouse's, the best way to protect your baby is to feed him only breast milk for the first six months. You might also watch what you eat yourself. During pregnancy and the first year after birth, you might completely avoid common allergens that are not essential to your diet, such as chocolate, and take only moderate amounts of others, such as citrus.

The key to a good breastfeeding diet—to *any* diet, perhaps—is moderation in everything. You might eat an orange for breakfast, for instance, instead of drinking a large glass of orange juice (which is equal to three or four oranges, but much lower in vitamins and fiber). You might have one chocolate instead of consuming the whole boxful, and eat only a small portion of beans, along with rice and meat, instead of a big bowlful of beans. You might change your protein sources frequently—rotating among meats, nuts, lentils, and cheeses, for example—since overeating one kind of food increases the chance of a reaction in your baby. Feed yourself as you will your growing child—on whole, minimally processed foods, in variety.

TESTING FOR FOOD ALLERGIES. The onset of your baby's reaction to something you've eaten ranges from thirty minutes to a day later. If you withdraw the offending substance from your diet, the baby's discomfort should begin to diminish within twenty-four hours. One way to identify offending foods is to withdraw all the most common allergens from your diet and see if your baby gets better. After a week or so, the improvement should be dramatic. At this point you can begin reintroducing the foods one at a time, a week or more apart, until you have identified the ones that bother your baby. If you suspect just one or two foods, perhaps because someone else in your family is sensitive to them, you may want to try eliminating these foods first. Or start with a dairy- and egg-free diet (see the chart), since cow's milk and eggs are two of the most common allergens. It's best however, to eliminate dairy products, eggs, *and* acidic fruits, *and* chocolate, *and* peanuts—all at once—since your baby may be reacting to two or more of these foods.

If you go on an elimination diet, make sure you find nutritionally adequate substitutes for the foods you're giving up. Some mothers of fussy babies haven't the time or energy to tend well to their own dietary needs. Putting an elimination diet on top of meal-skipping can be disastrous to your health. Before you go on such a diet, you might make up a ten-day menu, and buy all the groceries you'll need, freezing what won't keep.

If you plan to go without dairy products, in particular, then you will need to ensure that you're getting adequate calcium from other sources, such as a calcium supplement (which should be combined with magnesium, according to many nutritionists) or foods high in calcium, such as canned salmon and sardines, tofu, broccoli, almonds, kelp, and green leafy vegetables such as turnip greens and kale.

If you determine that cow's milk is the source of your baby's problem, it would be wise to check with a nutritionist about how best to meet your ongoing nutritional needs. Two federally funded programs, the Women, Infants and Children (WIC) Program and the Department of Agriculture's Cooperative Extension, offer nutritional information and planning services. Local offices of both agencies should be listed in your phone book.

"Sometimes I found that eating too much fruit, cabbage, or beans, or drinking too much juice, could cause an attack in my baby. I love fruit and did not realize that it could cause colic in a breastfed baby."

A DAIRY- AND EGG-FREE DIET

TYPE OF FOOD	FOODS YOU CAN EAT	FOODS TO AVOID FOR THE TEST
Milk	None	Milk (fresh, dried, condensed, evaporated, yogurt, buttermilk), "non-dairy" creamers containing caseinate
Meats, fish, poultry	All unprocessed meats	Creamed or breaded meats or fish, frankfurters and other processed meats with casein as an ingredient
Eggs	None	Any foods, including cakes, custards, pies, and meatloaf, that contain eggs
Cheese	No more than 2 oz. per day: blue cheese, Camembert, Cheddar, Colby, cream, Gouda, Swiss, Limburger, Parmesan, American	Cottage cheese
Breads and cereals	All milk-free breads and rolls, crackers and cooked cereals; some prepared cereals (check their labels for eggs and casein or other dairy products)	Bread, rolls, quick breads, and prepared mixes containing milk; French toast; zwieback and instant cereals containing milk or lactose
Soups	Broth, meat and vegetable varieties	Creamed soups
Other starches	Potatoes, sweet potatoes, pasta and noodles, rice, and other grains	Cream or cheese sauces, preparations with milk, instant potatoes, and milk-based gravy
Vegetables	Any fresh, frozen, or canned vegetables without added milk or lactose, and vegetable preparations without milk and butter	Cream or cheese sauces and preparations with milk or butter
Fruits	All kinds	Canned and frozen fruits or fruit products to which milk or lactose has been added
Desserts	Pies, cakes, and cookies made without butter or milk, and fruit ices made without milk (*Try freezing and then blending a banana for an ice cream substitute.*)	Ice cream, sherbet, custard, commercial sweet rolls, prepared mixes containing milk or lactose, and any other dessert made with milk products or served with whipped cream
Fats	Margarine, lard and other animal fats, peanut butter, sesame and nut butters, vegetable oils, olive oil and nut oils, dairy- and egg-free mayonnaise, non-dairy toppings containing no casein	Salad dressings containing cheese, yogurt, or buttermilk; butter and margarine-butter combinations; cream; sour cream; and yogurt
Beverages	Fruit juices	Milk, milkshakes, ice-cream sodas, hot cocoa, and coffee or tea with cream or milk
Sweets	Sugar, pure jellies and jams, honey, syrup, molasses, sugar candies	Candies containing milk or cream (milk chocolate, creams, nougat, caramels) or eggs

NOTE: This chart is adapted with permission from Julia A. Stockman, P.I. Nieburg, and F.A. Oski, *The Whole Pediatrician Catalog* (Philadelphia: W. B. Saunders, 1982).

MANAGING FOOD ALLERGIES. Having a baby with a food allergy doesn't necessarily mean you will have to live without that food until your baby is weaned. Every now and then you might try eating the bothersome food to see if your baby reacts. The baby may have a severe reaction when you stray from your diet just once, but, more likely, you will have to consume a large quantity of the food, or have it more than once or twice a week, to provoke a noticeable reaction. It's not easy to suddenly eliminate all dairy products, or eggs, or citrus fruits from your diet. You will slip now and then, and after you've done so a few times you will probably have an idea how much of the offending food you can safely eat, and how often you can eat it. Many mothers find they can have a little cheese every four or five days, or a bit of chocolate once a week, without the baby reacting much.

If your baby turns out to have multiple allergies, you might try a rotation diet. Limiting problem foods to once every other day, or every fifth day, may reduce your baby's symptoms while maintaining adequate nutrition for you.

Nonfood Allergies

Airborne as well as ingested substances can provoke allergic and hypersensitive reactions. Cigarette smoke is among the worst indoor pollutants, but others are house dust, mold, fungi, animal dander, and insect excrement. Cleaning products and building products—including carpeting, paint, particle board, and vinyl flooring—pollute the air in our houses with volatile organic compounds, all of which irritate mucous membranes, and some of which are carcinogenic besides. Babies may react strongly to any of countless airborne chemicals, such as hair spray, insecticidal spray, and the detergent in dishwasher steam.

Babies may also react to chemicals that touch their skin. Laying a baby on grass that has been treated with lawn chemicals can make him sick. The residue of fabric softener, laundry detergent, or dry-cleaning chemicals in clothing can cause rashes. Synthetic clothing or plastic can cause irritation where it rubs against the skin.

To reduce your baby's exposure to indoor pollutants, you'll want to limit your use of chemical cleaning and building products, and also spend plenty of time outdoors with your baby (assuming, of course, that the air isn't more polluted outdoors than indoors!). If your baby seems to be reacting to a nonfood substance, you may need the help of an allergist in identifying it. But since reducing a person's total exposure to allergens can enable him to tolerate some substances he couldn't before, you will probably want to try an elimination diet first.

CHAPTER EIGHT

Doctors, Disease, and Drugs

ALTHOUGH YOU MAY HAVE NO IDEA what is ailing your baby, you know by her cries when she is in pain. She grimaces or groans, lowers and furrows her brow, and squeezes her eyes shut. She opens her mouth wide with each cry, and you can see her arched, taut tongue inside. Her trunk and limbs are tense. She may seem pale, with damp palms, and the pupils of her eyes may be dilated more than normal. Her breathing and heart rate are faster than normal.

If your baby is suffering from pain that goes on day and night, it can disrupt her feeding, her sleeping, and her relationship with you. Pain may cause her to spit up more than usual and to vomit. If it is very severe, it may cause her to lose interest in sucking, thereby threatening her life.

Before pinning the label of colic on your crying baby, you'll want to be sure she doesn't have a problem that can be medically treated. If you haven't found an answer to her distress in chapter 6 or chapter 7, it is time for a visit to a doctor.

Finding a Physician to Help Your Baby

Your biggest hurdle may be finding a doctor who will take your baby's pain seriously. In the past, many medical professionals believed that babies didn't experience true pain. They thought babies to be too immature, with nervous systems too primitive to relay pain messages clearly. It's true that pain impulses travel more slowly in babies than they do in adults, which is why you sometimes know your baby is hurt before she does. It may also be true that babies can't localize pain—that they feel all pain in the abdominal region. But the main reason doctors have often discounted babies' pain is simply that babies can't verbalize their feelings. Since babies cry for many reasons and some cry much more than others, a doctor has great difficulty interpreting a particular baby's cries—at least during the typical ten-minute office visit.

Although medical professionals are increasingly aware that babies do feel pain, they don't always act on this awareness. Most hospitals and medical centers, for example, have strict regulations about humane and ethical care of adults and older children, but such standards are often lacking for conducting procedures, tests, and experiments on babies. Analgesia and anesthesia are often withheld from babies in circumcision and other surgery that would be considered very painful to older children and adults. In the case of circumcision, the doctor may not even tell the parents that the operation is totally unnecessary to a baby's well-being.

Even if a doctor can see that your baby is in distress, he or she may be of little help. Few physicians have been trained to deal with fussy babies. Most pediatric textbooks devote only a paragraph or two to excessive crying or colic, and every medical reference book lists different causes and cures.

Your physician may say you shouldn't worry, because your baby appears healthy, is gaining weight as expected, or isn't crying at the moment. The doctor may pat you on the back and reassure you that your baby's crying will lessen in a few weeks, and that you don't need to do anything about it. He or she may never even mention diagnostic procedures that might be valuable in uncovering the cause of your baby's pain.

Or maybe your doctor will have a ready answer for you. Without investigating the problem, the doctor may blame fussiness on your milk or on your baby's present formula. If your milk is supposedly at fault, you're told to try formula; if you're using formula already, you're to try a *different* formula.

If changing the menu doesn't help and you insist something is wrong, the doctor may diagnose colic, and prescribe drugs to stop the crying. But such drugs only mask a baby's pain, and they can be dangerous.

If you've had any of these experiences, you probably should consider changing doctors. You don't have to stay with a physician who doesn't take your concerns seriously.

To find a doctor you can trust, ask your obstetrician or midwife, a

"The pediatricians in my community are all very unskilled at helping parents who have babies with colic. The doctor may see the baby a couple of times, but he's soon at the end of his rope. Either he'll say, 'This is colic and you've got to live with it,' or he'll suggest using medication. If the mother is breastfeeding the baby, he'll say, 'Let's start formula.'"

local La Leche League leader, or your childbirth educator for recommendations. You may want a pediatrician—a specialist in diseases of childhood—or you may prefer a family practitioner who has had a lot of experience with infants. If your baby's problems seem severe and local doctors don't appear to have any answers, you may want to consider locating an infant specialist in a medical school or teaching hospital. Pediatric gastroenterologists (G.I. specialists) and pediatric allergists work with severe cases of infant distress, especially when the problems seem to be digestion- or allergy-related. Don't be afraid to ask the doctor about his or her experience and philosophy on the phone before scheduling an exam.

CHECKLIST FOR EVALUATING A BABY DOCTOR

✔ You should feel confident that your baby's physician has up-to-date knowledge and plenty of experience concerning the many causes of infant pain.

✔ He or she should refrain from giving you pat answers that don't help, or prescribing drugs that simply mask your baby's discomfort.

✔ The doctor should listen well. He or she should treat your baby's crying as important, and your perceptions and opinions about your baby as valuable in uncovering solutions.

✔ You shouldn't feel rushed with your appointment or have to wait long to see the doctor.

✔ Your physician should be readily available to talk by telephone.

✔ Your doctor should welcome your seeking a second opinion, especially if he or she has recommended extensive tests.

✔ You should feel that no stone has been left unturned to discover what is causing your baby's pain.

Your Baby's Physical Examination

A doctor's examination of your baby should include listening to your baby's heart and lungs with a stethoscope (to screen for heart and lung defects); examination of your baby's mouth (to rule out thrush, cleft palate, and an overly tight frenulum, the connective tissue under the tongue that may cause a baby to be tongue-tied and thus interfere with nursing); a look into the ear canals, preferably using a pneumatic otoscope, tympanometry, or reflectometry (to check for middle ear infection); examination of your baby's collar bone (to rule out a broken clavicle), hip joints (to rule out a dislocated hip), abdomen and testicles (to rule out an inguinal or hiatal hernia), and bottom and anus (to screen for diaper rash, a too-small anal opening, or an anal fissure); and a urinalysis (to rule out urinary tract infection). Most important, the doctor should ask for details about your family history, especially concerning allergies, and about the symptoms your baby has been showing.

Illnesses You Should Know about

Before the baby's examination you should have made detailed mental notes (or even written notes) about the baby's symptoms, especially as they might relate to the following conditions.

DIARRHEA. It's not unusual for first-time mothers to think their breastfed babies have diarrhea when they really don't. The stools of a fully breastfed baby are usually runny, and they are often as numerous as six to eight a day. They are characteristically yellow, and their aroma is normally quite mild and inoffensive.

If your baby has diarrhea, she may have as many as twelve to sixteen stools a day. They will probably smell bad, and they may contain mucus or even tiny flecks of blood. They will probably be darker than normal stools, green or even brownish. The time to worry is when your baby's stools become continual, when they smell bad, and when she acts sick or has a fever.

The primary danger of diarrhea is dehydration, the severe loss of

HOW TO DESCRIBE YOUR BABY'S SYMPTOMS TO THE DOCTOR

BABY'S SYMPTOMS	HOW TO DESCRIBE THEM
PAIN CRIES	
Your baby seems whiny and cries frequently day and night. No change in position seems to help.	"She seems to have *chronic* pain."
Your baby's pain attacks are sharp and sudden; she suddenly gasps and lets out a loud, piercing scream.	"She has *acute* pain attacks."
LOCATION OF PAIN	
When you rotate your baby's ear, pressing it gently with your fingertips in a rhythmical, circular motion, she fusses or bats at your hand.	"It seems to be coming from her left [or right] ear."
Your baby appears to have pain in the hip joint when you bend her leg.	"It seems to hurt her hip when her left [or right] leg is bent" (a sign of dislocation).
REDNESS	
Unusual redness or heat comes from a spot on the baby's body during a crying attack.	"Her ear seems hot." "Her abdomen feels hot." "His left [or right] testicle feels hot."
SWELLING	
Your baby has a swelling or puffy area on her body.	"Her temples seem swollen." "Her abdomen gets [or stays] distended." "His left [or right] testicle gets swollen when he cries."
TIMING OF CRIES	
A record of your baby's crying over several days shows distinct patterns.	"She cries in cycles for about half an hour every two hours." "She cries every evening as though she is in severe pain, usually beginning around 5:00 P.M. and ending about midnight." "She wakes up abruptly during the night with screams of pain unrelated to hunger."
FEVER	
The baby feels hot. *(Call the doctor about any fever if the baby is under three months old.)*	"Her rectal temperature at 10:00 P.M. was 102°F. At midnight it was 103°."
STOOLS	
Your baby has more, or fewer, bowel movements than usual, and their smell or color changes. *(For severe diarrhea call the doctor immediately; see page 000.)*	*For constipation:* "Her stools are hard, like small pebbles, and leave no trace on the diaper." *For diarrhea:* "Her stools are liquid and greenish." "She had six bowel movements yesterday; usually she has just two." "She seems to have mild diarrhea all the time." "Her stools have flecks of mucus, [blood, undigested food] in them." *(Tip: Bring a recently soiled diaper with you.)*

HOW TO DESCRIBE YOUR BABY'S SYMPTOMS TO THE DOCTOR—*Continued*

BABY'S SYMPTOMS	HOW TO DESCRIBE THEM

VOMITING AND SPITTING UP

Your baby throws up frequently and forcefully, or spits up more than usual.	"She has *projectile vomiting* after every feeding—it shoots across the room." "She vomits during sleep, leaving a wet patch on the sheet." "Her vomit is white [yellow, brown, green]." "Her vomit has flecks of blood in it" (or "her vomit looks like coffee grounds"). "She seems to feel better after she has vomited," (or "she doesn't seem to feel better after vomiting"). "She coughs or chokes over and over after she spits up." *(Tip: Take a sample of your baby's vomit on a diaper with you.)*

BREATHING

Your baby's breathing is noisy, extra fast, or difficult, or it stops more than momentarily. (Note: When babies are in active sleep, they often suck their tongues, groan, sigh, and make other noises.)	"She is *wheezing*" (making a sound like the purr of a cat from her throat or chest). "She is breathing very fast" (or "she is taking very rapid, shallow breaths"). "She is having trouble getting air in and out." "Her nostrils flare and the center of her chest sinks in with each breath" (this could indicate pneumonia). "She stops breathing for minutes at a time" (this is *apnea*).

bodily fluids. Signs to watch for in both breastfed and bottle-fed babies are—

1. The baby goes for many hours without wetting.
2. Her mouth seems dry instead of being moist.
3. Her breathing is fast and heavy.

Should all three of these signs appear together, seek medical attention immediately. Fortunately, life-threatening diarrhea is very rare in totally breastfed babies.

Diarrhea often signals that a baby is coming down with an infection. It can also be one of a cluster of symptoms caused by a reaction to formula or a substance in breast milk. An allergic breastfed baby may have consistently green stools with flecks of mucus in them. Other allergy symptoms are irritability, gas, vomiting, stuffy nose, rattly breathing or wheezing, and rashes (see chapter 7, "The Colic-Allergy Connection"). A breastfed baby with diarrhea may also be reacting to a drug or some other substance that her mother is ingesting.

Diarrhea is *not* a sign to discontinue breastfeeding in favor of other fluids. Breast milk is by far the most balanced, readily absorbable liquid your baby can have during an illness.

FEVER. In older babies a fever as high as 105 degrees should not, by itself, be a cause for alarm; it is probably caused by a minor viral or bacterial infection, and is a sign that the body's defense mechanisms are working. If the child is seriously ill, there will be other disturbing symptoms, such as listlessness and confusion, that will warn you to call a doctor.

In babies under three months, however, fever is rare and legitimately worrisome. If your baby is under three months old and has *any* fever, you should consult a doctor right away. A baby born in a hospital may have contracted an infection there—from an intervention during labor or delivery (such as internal fetal monitoring) or after birth (such as circumcision), or from the germs of hospital patients. Or the infection may be related to a prenatal or hereditary condition.

If your baby has had a shot recently, fever may be a reaction to the inoculation (see page 109).

A baby's temperature may also be elevated simply because she is overdressed. Unless you are outdoors with the baby in cold weather, she shouldn't be tightly wrapped in heavy clothing and blankets. If the baby already has a temperature, overdressing her will only make it rise higher, and it may result in life-threatening heatstroke.

How do you take a baby's temperature? Most people take it rectally, but this can be scary for the parents and maddening for the baby. Dr. Robert Mendelsohn advises taking an axillary (underarm) temperature instead (in babies axillary temperatures usually vary only slightly from either oral or rectal readings).[98] Digital thermometers, by the way, are much easier to read than the old-fashioned kind.

What should you do to reduce a child's fever? Normally, you shouldn't even try. People used to give children aspirin for fevers, but aspirin has been associated with Reye's syndrome, which can be fatal. Most doctors today instead recommend acetaminophen (for example, Tylenol), but medications really aren't necessary; in fact, they can do more harm than good. **Reducing a fever artificially can actually prolong the disease.**

If you can't just let the fever run its course, sponge the baby with lukewarm water (not cold water or alcohol).

THRUSH. A yeast infection in the baby's mouth and gastrointestinal tract may make her fussy and reluctant to nurse. She may have white spots that look like cheese curds on the insides of her lips and cheeks, on her tongue, on the roof of her mouth, and on her gums. She may also have a diaper rash that looks like a mild burn or just a patch of red dots, and doesn't respond to the usual treatment. Your nipples may be pink, itchy, and flaky, or red and burning; they may be swollen or cracked.

Sometimes babies pick up yeast infections in their passage through the birth canal; this is common when the mother is diabetic. Thrush also often occurs after the baby or mother has had a course of antibiotics, since these drugs kill bacteria that normally control the growth of yeast.

Thrush is usually treated with nystatin suspension, for which a prescription is required. Improvement is usually immediate; your baby may be happy and ready to nurse minutes after you give her the medication (half a dropperful on each side of the mouth, four times a day). The treatment should be continued, however, for fourteen days, or the white patches will probably reappear.

Even if your nipples aren't sore, they should be treated at the same time. Some women daub the liquid nystatin on their nipples, but nystatin ointment is probably more effective. The ointment can also be applied to the baby's bottom.

URINARY PROBLEMS. Infections in a baby's urinary tract can cause pain and colic-like crying. Symptoms of urinary tract infections may include a sudden increase or decrease in diaper-wetting frequency (newborns normally wet as many as a hundred diapers a week), urine that smells bad, a flushed face or excessive straining when urinating (slight trembling is normal in some babies, especially girls), and jaundice that doesn't go away. More often, however, there are only vague symptoms, such as diarrhea, vomiting, fever, fatigue, poor appetite, and irritability.

A doctor can find out if your baby has a urinary tract infection by testing her urine. A small plastic bag is taped around her genitals, or urine is caught in a container as she urinates.

If the specimen tests positive, antibiotics are prescribed.

In some cases, painful urination is caused by an inflammation of the penis end in boys who haven't been circumcised. This usually occurs when parents try to pull back a baby's foreskin to clean under-

POSSIBLE CAUSES OF A BABY'S PAIN

PROBLEM	DESCRIPTION	SYMPTOMS	TREATMENT
COMMON CAUSES			
Food intolerance (see chapter 7, "The Colic-Allergy Connection")	A breastfed baby may react to any of various substances in the mother's diet. A bottle-fed baby may react to cow's milk sugar or proteins, or to soy proteins in formula.	Crying between feedings, swollen and tender belly, gas, vomiting, frothy or green stools, poor weight gain, skin rash, runny or stuffy nose.	A breastfeeding mother may need to go on an elimination diet. A bottle-fed baby may need a special non-allergenic formula, such as Progestimil or Nutramigen.
Ear infection (see pages 111–13)	Inflammation and fluid buildup in the middle ear. Rare in newborns.	Often occurs 7 to 10 days after the onset of a cold. Slow weight gain may be the only symptom in very young babies.	Doctor may prescribe a course of antibiotics.
Respiratory infection	A baby may catch a bacterial or viral infection in the hospital or from a family member.	Fever, stuffy or runny nose, pallor, irritability, diarrhea, hoarseness, coughing, sneezing.	Any baby under three months of age who has a fever should be seen by a doctor. Treatment depends on the diagnosis.
Circumcision	Babies suffer pain during circumcision, when no pain relief is provided, and for about 4 days afterward.	Crying, fussiness, "shutdown," especially if no anesthesia has been used.	Refuse circumcision, or insist on local anesthesia. To protect the wound from chafing and urine, wrap the end of the penis with a strip of gauze covered with petroleum jelly.
Vaccination reaction (see page 109)	Reaction to the DPT shot or another vaccine.	Fussiness, slight fever, swelling at injection site. More severe reactions include high fever, high-pitched cry, "shutdown," convulsion.	Doctor may suggest acetaminophen or other fever- and pain-reducing medication. The pertussis component can be omitted from future vaccinations.

POSSIBLE CAUSES OF A BABY'S PAIN—*Continued*

PROBLEM	DESCRIPTION	SYMPTOMS	TREATMENT
Anal fissure, constriction, or inflammation	Bowel movements hurt because of soreness or tightness in the anus.	The anus may have a small sore, a fissure; it may be inflamed from a strep infection or diarrhea; or it may be too tight.	Doctor may recommend a suppository or ointment.
Gastrocolic reflex	When food enters the stomach, a hormone is released that causes the colon to contract.	The baby stops in the middle of a feeding to cry for several minutes, but has no diarrhea or vomiting.	Wait for a few minutes until the cramping goes away, and then resume feeding.

RARER CAUSES

PROBLEM	DESCRIPTION	SYMPTOMS	TREATMENT
Urinary tract infection (see page 99)	Urinary tube or organs are inflamed.	The baby cries inconsolably and seems to have abdominal pain. Other signs: a change in wetting frequency, a stop-start pattern of wetting, urine that smells bad, straining to urinate.	Urinalysis will determine if antibiotics or other intervention is needed.
Fractured clavicle	The baby's collarbone may have been broken during birth as her shoulders squeezed forward.	The baby may want to nurse on one side only and may cry when moved. You may be able to feel a small lump where the bone is beginning to heal.	The bone is normally allowed to heal on its own.
Dislocated hip	The baby's thigh bone may be partly pulled from its socket at birth. This is most common in breech and cesarean births.	The baby cries inconsolably until the dislocation is treated. She may seem to dislike cuddling and movement, especially of her lower body.	This is normally diagnosed at birth by moving the hips. Ultrasound is the most accurate diagnostic tool. Splinting may be necessary.

Continued on next page

Possible Causes of a Baby's Pain—*Continued*

Problem	Description	Symptoms	Treatment
Hematoma	The baby has a dome-shaped swelling where blood has collected under the skin because of birth injury.	Temporary pain and crying.	The baby may need to be hospitalized for observation.
Heart defect	The baby may have a heart valve defect or a heart rhythm disorder.	The baby may fatigue quickly, breathe rapidly, have a bluish cast to the skin, resist lying on her back, or have an abnormally fast heart rate. Some babies show no symptoms initially.	The baby may need to be hospitalized for observation and, possibly, corrective surgery.
Transient nervous system immaturity	Some babies, particularly those who are premature, experience temporary delays in nervous system functioning. They usually outgrow this within about four months.	Poor sucking skills, extreme muscle tension, *hypertonia* (the baby may arch her back or extend her arms and legs abnormally), *hypotonia* (she may be limp, like a rag doll).	The baby can be helped in feeding and other matters by a physical or occupational therapist who is specially trained to work with infants.
Gastroesophageal reflux (GER) (see pages 58–59)	The sphincter at the esophagus end of the stomach is lax, allowing excessive regurgitation.	Crying and irritability at feeding time; spitting up and vomiting. Frequent night waking with small, wet patches of vomit under the baby's face. Vomit may have flecks of blood in it. Other possible symptoms include coughing, stuffy nose, wheezing, and periods of apnea (breathing stoppage). Some babies arch their backs or throw their heads back during feedings.	Usually clears up by 18 months. Keep the baby upright after feeding, in a car seat or infant seat. The doctor may prescribe antacids, thickened formula, or, rarely, corrective surgery if the condition doesn't clear up over time, or if a hiatal hernia is involved.

neath. The foreskin should be left alone until it becomes loose enough to retract easily, usually by the time a boy is three or four years old. Forcing the foreskin back earlier can cause the penis tip to become strangulated by a tight ring of skin.

In circumcised boys, a swollen, red area on the tip of the glans may be caused by diaper chafing or ammonia. To prevent this, change wet diapers promptly—before they start smelling of ammonia—and make sure the diapers aren't too rough.

Drugged Babies

When a doctor can't readily identify the cause of a baby's distress, he or she may choose just to treat the symptoms. Some doctors simply prescribe a drug that will deaden the baby's pain and help her to sleep.

Unfortunately, the science of medicating small babies is still quite primitive. It is estimated that only one-fourth of drugs currently being used to treat babies have undergone adequate evaluation.[99] Drugs are tested on adults and older children, not young babies. And a newborn's body doesn't work quite the same way as a child's or adult's. Her digestion takes longer, her blood circulates differently, and she has a higher proportion of body fluid and a lower proportion of body fat than older children and adults have. Her liver and kidneys, as well as her stomach and intestines, are immature.

For these reasons young babies, especially those born prematurely, can't process drugs well. A baby's ability to metabolize drugs increases as she gets older. When she is several months old, her body will be much better able to deal with drugs. But by then, of course, the colic will probably have passed.

The most commonly used medications for colic cause the muscles in the baby's digestive system to relax, break up and diminish gas, or sedate the baby. All colic drugs can have side effects. Sometimes a baby has what is called a "paradoxical" reaction to a drug meant to make her sleep. Rather than becoming calm and sleepy, as her parents hoped, she becomes hyperactive, staying awake all night in a drugged frenzy. Babies can also have hangovers from drugs. A drug that makes a baby sleepy at night may make her inconsolable by morning. And sedatives can be dangerous for babies. When a baby has been given too much, her breathing may slow down, her pulse may be altered, and her central nervous system, which oversees her

Drugs Commonly Used to Treat Colic

Generic Name	Common Names	Uses	Possible Side Effects*
antacids	Maalox, sodium bicarbonate	Neutralizes digestive acids and reduces heartburn.	In adults: nausea, elevated blood pressure, and fluid retention. Side effects in infants are unknown.
antihistamine	Phenergan Syrup	Makes the baby drowsy.	Extreme drowsiness, dizziness, seizures, coma. Not for use in children under 2 years.
atropine	belladonna, Donnagel, Lomotil, Donnatal, Bellergal	Relaxes digestive tract and sedates the baby.	Rapid heartbeat, constipation, difficult urination, headache, extreme drowsiness and dulling of senses, dry, hot skin, restlessness, impaired intestinal motility, elevated white blood cell count, delirium, coma. Not recommended for infants under 6 months.
barbiturate	Phenobarbital, Donnatal	Makes the baby drowsy and sluggish.	Extreme drowsiness, irritability, hyperactivity, nausea, breathing stoppage, cognitive deficits.
diphenhydramine	Benadryl	Induces sleep and relieves allergic symptoms.	Central nervous system depression, restlessness, changes in the blood, thickening of mucous secretions, vomiting, constipation or diarrhea, dry mouth.
codeine	Calcidrine Syrup	A narcotic pain killer.	Constipation, abdominal pain, vomiting, nausea, central nervous system and respiratory depression.
paregoric	Donnagel-PG	Relieves intestinal cramping.	Drowsiness, lightheadedness, sweating, constipation, dizziness, nausea, vomiting, addiction.

Drugs Commonly Used to Treat Colic—*Continued*

Generic Name	Common Names	Uses	Possible Side Effects*
dicyclomine hydrochloride	Bentyl Di-Spaz	Relieves spasms in the gastrointestinal tract.	Dry mouth, urine retention, rapid heartbeat, constipation, headache, nausea, vomiting, breathlessness, breathing stoppage, suffocation, seizures, muscular rigidity, susceptibility to heat stroke, coma, death. Not for use in infants under 6 months.
simethicone	Mylicon, Mylanta, Colicon Drops	Defoaming agent that breaks down gas bubbles in the digestive system.	None known.

SOURCES: H. W. Griffith, *Complete Guide to Prescription and Nonprescription Drugs* (Los Angeles: Body Press, 1989); J. W. Long, *The Essential Guide to Prescription Drugs* (New York: Harper and Row, 1982); W. Benitz and D. Tatro, *Pediatric Drug Handbook* (Chicago:Yearbook Medical Publishers, 1981); *Physician's Desk Reference* (Medical Economics Data, 1991); M. Levine et al., *Developmental Behavioral Pediatrics* (Philadelphia: W. B. Saunders, 1983); L. A. Robinson and A. L. Brown, "Colic: Pharmaceutical and Medical Intervention," *Pediatric Nursing* 5 (1979): 61–64; S. P. Rubin and M. Prendergast, "Infantile Colic: Incidence and Treatment in a Norfolk Community," *Child Care, Health and Development* 10 (1984):219–21; M. Stahlberg, "Infantile Colic: Occurrence and Risk Factors," *European Journal of Pediatrics* 143 (1984):108–11; C. Wood and J. Walker-Smith, eds., *MacKeith's Infant Feeding and Feeding Difficulties* (New York: Churchill-Livingston, 1981); R. A. Cockington, N. Don, and L. Gilbert, "Use of Medication in Infancy," *Australian Pediatrics Journal* 17 (1981):216–18; P. J. White, "Management of Infantile Colic," *American Journal of Diseases of Children* 133 (1979):995–1001; and J. C. O'Donovan and A. S. Brandstock, "The Failure of Conventional Drug Therapy in the Management of Infantile Colic," *American Journal of Diseases of Children* 133 (1979):999–1001.

*Most of the side effects listed here have been observed in studies on adults and older children. Research on drug effects in infants is sparse and inconclusive.

bodily functions, may be severely affected. (See "Folk Remedies for Colic," page 81.)

Dicyclomine (Bentyl) is the only drug that has been approved by the U.S. Food and Drug Administration (FDA) as possibly helping babies with colic. It works by relaxing the baby's intestinal muscles, inhibiting painful spasms. At the time of FDA approval, dicyclomine's known side effects included dry mouth, dizziness, sluggishness, loss of appetite, constipation, rashes, and urine retention. A more serious side effect was discovered later, when manufacturers reported two incidents of respiratory failure in babies who had been given the drug. Two years later there were other reports of death, breathing stoppage, seizures, and coma in babies who were given dicyclomine. Now the drug is recommended only for babies over six months of age.[100]

Phenobarbital, the most commonly prescribed sedative for crying and irritable babies, has been found to *increase* infants' irritability.[101]

Drugs that should never be given babies as treatment for colic include Dramamine (dimenhydrinate), Donnatal (a combination of phenobarbital, hyoscyamine sulfate, atropine sulfate, and scopolamine hydrobomide), and drugs in the phenothiazine family, which are sometimes used to treat flu-like infections, coughs, and allergies. These drugs have been associated with near-fatal reactions.[102]

Fortunately, parents are often very reluctant to administer drugs prescribed for their fussy babies. In one survey, all but five of thirty-five mothers of colicky babies were found to be in frank despair about their babies' problems. Each of the thirty-five had consulted a physician, and each was given a prescription for drugs. Every mother expressed ambivalence about using a drug on her baby. And all but one mother promptly discontinued using the drugs after giving their babies only one or two doses.[103]

CHAPTER NINE

Your Fussy Older Baby,
Your Cranky Toddler

THE EARLIER CHAPTERS of this book have focused on the young baby, under three months in age. As a baby gets older he still cries, though usually somewhat less. His complaints may now be a little easier to identify.

Your Crying Older Baby

Once feedings problems have been resolved and colic has peaked, your baby may cry for new reasons. He may catch his first cold, and, if you and he are unlucky, the cold may lead to his first ear infection. With the ear infection could come the most acute pain he will have yet experienced. Your baby will probably also get his first vaccination, and he may have a reaction to it. When he starts to eat solid foods, he is likely to have some bouts with diaper rash. And about the same time he starts on solids, your baby will, more or less painfully, cut his first tooth. Soon thereafter, he will probably begin to cry from a fear of being separated from you, and he just won't be himself as long as you are away.

SEPARATION ANXIETY. By about eight months of age your baby will have become so attached to you that he cries every time you leave his sight. Suddenly he knows how much he needs you, yet he hasn't yet learned that when you go away you always come back. He may be able to assuage his fear by crawling after you from room to room, but if he can't keep up you'll have to carry him with you. If you can't carry him, tell him when you're leaving ("I'm going to the bathroom—I'll be right back") and when you've returned ("Here I am!"). If you sneak off when he isn't looking, he'll only become more anxious, vigilant, and tearful.

At about one year of age, your baby may begin to fear strangers. If you leave him with a babysitter he doesn't know, he will feel totally bereft. This phase will be easier for both of you if your baby has had a chance to develop a strong attachment to someone besides yourself. Then, when you must leave him for an hour or a day, he can find some consolation in the arms of his father, grandparent, or special friend.

TEETHING. The first tooth usually erupts when a baby is about six months old, though it is entirely normal for this to happen at any time during the first year. A baby may experience symptoms of teething—fussiness, drooling, chewing on things, appetite loss, and restless nights—as long as four months before a tooth comes in. So between about three months and two years—the average age at which the second set of molars comes in—a baby is teething all the time.

The discomfort of teething varies a lot—from one baby to another, from one tooth to another, and from one day to the next. Sucking may temporarily increase gum swelling and make a baby more uncomfortable, which is why his appetite may suffer sometimes. The worst pain is probably just as the teeth are cutting through, when the gums are quite swollen and inflamed. Babies seem to experience the most discomfort with molars, as their broad top surface cuts through.

Many parents believe teething causes runny noses, fevers, and diarrhea, but most doctors disagree. Still, the loss of appetite and wakefulness due to teething may in turn cause some digestive disturbance (and hence runny stools) and a lowered resistance to infection.

Most babies with teething pain enjoy chewing on firm plastic toys, including water-filled rings that can be chilled in the refrigerator. Your baby may also like sucking on an ice cube wrapped in a clean cloth, or chewing on dry toast. He may like you to massage his gums (or he may hate this). Some parents use over-the-counter gum-numbing medications, which contain a mild anesthetic; these are probably safe if used only occasionally.

VACCINATIONS. If your baby is like most, he'll soon endure quite a few inoculations. The diphtheria, pertussis, and tetanus (DPT) vaccine is normally given three times in the first year, beginning at two months of age; the oral polio vaccine is given twice, and the measles, mumps, and rubella (MMR) vaccine once. Boosters of all these vaccines are given around fifteen months and again before a child starts school. Vaccinations are the main event of most "well-baby" exams, and are therefore the pediatrician's bread and butter. Although more and more parents are refusing the vaccines for their children, most comply, since a complete immunization record is generally required for admission to school.

Vaccinations are intended to provide immunity to potentially serious diseases. However, the full effects of injecting various foreign antigens into a baby's body are still uncertain. Some renegade doctors believe vaccines weaken the immune system, making a child vulnerable to recurrent respiratory infections and perhaps even to auto-immune diseases like cancer and leukemia. Serious direct reactions to vaccines, though very rare, include epilepsy, mental retardation, learning disabilities, and paralysis. Immediate reactions such as fevers, long screaming bouts, "shutdown," and painful swellings are quite common, especially following administration of the controversial pertussis (whooping cough) vaccine.

The aim of mass inoculations is to eliminate certain diseases entirely. According to Dr. Robert Mendelsohn, however, "there is no convincing scientific evidence that mass inoculations can be credited with eliminating any childhood disease."[104] Some infectious diseases have declined dramatically in incidence and virulence in countries both with and without mass inoculation programs.

No one can be sure whether vaccines provide lasting immunity. During disease outbreaks, many—sometimes most—of the victims have been immunized. In fact, doctors' efforts to reduce the incidence of relatively harmless childhood diseases is causing an increase in the frequency of these diseases among adults, in whom they can be much more serious.

For these reasons decisions about vaccinations—which ones to give a child and when—are difficult, yet parents feel pressured to make them very soon after a birth. You *can* delay a bit, however, while you research the risks and benefits of the various vaccines (see "Recommended Reading"). A few doctors actually prefer to delay shots until a baby is at least six months old, when his immune and nervous systems are better developed. And keep in mind that components of a shot can be administered separately; for instance, if you're worried about the pertussis vaccine, or your baby has already had a frightening reaction to it, he can receive a DT shot (diphtheria and tetanus, without pertussis) instead. Dr. Randall Neustaedter points out that of the diseases which the DPT shot is meant to prevent, only pertussis commonly causes problems within a child's first year. "If you decide not to give that vaccine because of its associated dangers," he advises, "then there is no harm in delaying other immunizations until your child is beyond infancy and less vulnerable to side effects of the shots"—that is, until your child is about two years old.[105]

Refusing shots doesn't necessarily mean your child can never go to school. All states grant medical exemptions to vaccinations (a waver must be signed by a physician), and almost all grant exemptions on the basis of the parents' religious or philosophical beliefs. The pertussis vaccine, because it is so dangerous, is not required at all in some states.

When you do take your child for a shot, make sure he is well; in fact, you should probably postpone the vaccination if another family member has a cold or flu. This way you'll avoid putting added strain on his immune system.

Nursing your baby during a shot may distract him somewhat from the pain. To help prevent swelling and inflammation, gently massage the injection site, as you hold a cotton wad against it, immediately after the shot.

Your doctor may recommend acetaminophen for pain and fever after a vaccination.

COLDS. If your magical milk and colostrum have kept your baby in perfect health throughout the early months, his first cold may come as a dismaying surprise. He isn't pretty with snot on his face, and he probably acts miserable.

Colds are hard on babies, because they are instinctive nose breathers. If a baby can't breathe through his nose he can't nurse, and he can't sleep either. But he needs to nurse *and* sleep, of course, to get well.

If your baby has a cold, keep him home and quiet and warm (but don't overdress him if he's feverish). Give him plenty of breast milk or other fluids. To help him breathe easier, humidify the bedroom with a cold-water humidifier (be sure to clean it daily) or place a pan of water on top of the radiator or woodstove. If he is very stuffed up, take him into the bathroom, close the door, and run hot water in the shower for twenty minutes or so as he breathes the steamy air.

You can also thin the mucus in the baby's nose with salt water. Stir 1/4 teaspoon salt into a cup of boiled water, and let the mixture cool, or buy saline solution ready-made in a drugstore. Holding the baby's hands over his head as he lies on his back, drip a few drops of salt water from a medicine dropper into his nose (*don't* use a spray bottle).

After a minute or two, you can remove the thinned mucus with a rubber ear bulb-syringe. Squeeze the bulb, insert the tip into a nostril, and slowly release the bulb as you withdraw the tip. You can also use the bulb syringe without the salt water, though this is less effective.

If these measures don't work, or you're too sleepy to try them, just hold the baby upright so his nasal passages can drain. You can sleep, propped with pillows or in an armchair, with the baby against your chest. It's more comfortable, at least, than listening to screaming all night.

EAR INFECTIONS. According to one survey, *otitis media*, or inflammation of the middle ear, is the most frequently diagnosed childhood illness.[106] An earache is most often a complication of a cold, but ear infections can arise spontaneously, and for many children they are a chronic problem during the early years.

Certain children are more prone to ear infections than others. Those who have allergies, or have allergic family members, are especially likely to have inflamed middle ears, as are children who have been fed solid foods or cow's milk (even if only in formula) in the early months. Children whose parents smoke develop ear infections at a much higher rate than do children in homes without smokers; poorly ventilated woodstoves, too, can make children prone to ear infections. Children with nutritional deficiencies are at risk for developing *otitis media*. So are children who spend time in group day care, which makes them more likely to develop illnesses of all types. And babies who are given bottles while they lie on their backs are likely to develop persistent fluid in the middle ear, since the horizontal position makes it easy for the milk to back up the Eustachian tube, where it can become a medium for bacterial growth.

Although chronic middle ear inflammation can occur without much pain, acute ear infections are often very painful. Typically, the infection sets in just as a baby is getting over a cold. The baby feels worst at nighttime, since pressure on the eardrum is greatest when he lies down. He usually sleeps fitfully, and acts fussy and clingy. He may run a fever, and he may refuse to nurse on one side. The doctor may ask if the baby has been pulling or poking at his ear, but most babies with ear infections don't do this.

Ear infections are usually diagnosed by looking at the eardrum with an otoscope (more sophisticated diagnostic tools are pneumatic otoscopes, *tympanometry*, and *reflectometry*). Inexpensive otoscopes are available at pharmacies and through some mail-order catalogs for home use, but using them takes some practice, and is especially difficult if the baby objects. Once you do get a look at the eardrum, you will probably have difficulty interpreting what you see. You might ask your doctor for guidance.

Although ear infections rarely cause permanent hearing loss, they often affect a child's hearing temporarily. Children with chronic ear infections, in fact, may experience diminished hearing for months. Whether this can have a permanent effect on their mental and linguistic development is unknown. (Some studies have shown an association between chronic ear infections and delayed development, but this doesn't mean ear infections necessarily *cause* the developmental delay.)

The conventional treatment for ear infections is a ten-day course of antibiotics. When they work, antibiotics seem like miracle drugs. But they do have adverse side effects: (1) they kill "good" intestinal bacteria, essential for proper digestion and immune function, as well as "bad" bacteria; (2) they increase susceptibility to intestinal infection by organisms such as *Candida albicans* and *Giardia*; (3) they can cause the lining of the intestine to thin, increasing the likelihood a child will develop food allergies (see page 87); (4) they may reduce the absorption of certain nutrients; and (5) with overuse they promote the development of antibiotic-resistant bacteria.[107]

In *Childhood Ear Infections*, Michael Schmidt cites substantial evidence that antibiotics do not generally speed recovery from ear infections and that giving antibiotics early in the course of an infection can lead to recurrent ear infections.[108] "It appears that when treatment is delayed," says Schmidt, "children are able to develop natural immunity, thereby insulating them from future episodes. Early antibiotic therapy appears to inhibit the initial response."[109] Antibiotics certainly do no good where the ear is inflamed but not infected, as is the case with many allergic children.

When one antibiotic doesn't work, a doctor usually prescribes another. Soon a family may have several bottles of bubble gum—flavored medicine in the refrigerator—and a baby who seems as sick as ever, perhaps with a chronic cold as well as recurrent ear infections. At this point the child may undergo *tympanostomy*, the surgical insertion of tubes in the eardrum. The surgery is expensive and requires general anesthesia, but it does reduce middle ear pressure, allow fluid to drain, and improve hearing for a few months. However, the insertion of tubes may also cause *tympanosclerosis* (formation of hard, dense tissue around the bones of the middle ear), and, according to one researcher, tubes "may be associated with a long-term risk of hearing loss."[110]

If antibiotics work for a short time but the infections keep recurring, *prophylactic* (preventive) treatment with antibiotics may be prescribed. In other words, the baby is given daily doses of an antibiotic over a period of several months, in the hope of preventing reinfection.

Are there any alternatives to antibiotics and surgery? Some parents treat ear infections by placing a warm, carefully monitored heating pad under the baby's ear, by dropping warm olive oil or herbal drops into the ear, by giving the baby acetaminophen, and by keeping him upright. Many parents swear by homeopathic remedies, which, if they won't cure the ear infection, at least will do no harm. (Homeopathic remedies are available from physicians who practice homeopathy and from several mail-order companies. Some are also sold in health-food stores, but these may be of too low a potency to be effective.)

In the case of chronic ear infections, the underlying causes—whether allergy, nutritional deficiency, or biomechanical obstruction—should be identified and treated.

DIAPER RASH. As long as a baby is fed only breast milk, urine and feces are usually mild and nonirritating. But when a baby starts on solids, occasional diaper rash becomes likely. At any given time, as many as one out of three nine- to twelve-month-olds have diaper rash.

Diaper rash is usually caused by a chemical reaction when a baby's stool mixes with urine. Digestive enzymes in the stool break down the skin, and infection can then set in. Babies are much more likely to get diaper rash when they have had diarrhea or an illness. New foods and chafing of the diaper play a part, too.

The best way to prevent diaper rash is to get soiled diapers off your baby as quickly as possible. Once redness appears, thickly apply protective ointment (such as Desitin, Eucerin, or Vaseline) over the baby's bottom to prevent further skin breakdown. See your doctor if your baby's skin begins to look infected. Ordinary diaper rash can quickly become infected with yeast or another pathogen.

According to pediatric dermatologists, the best way to clean your baby's bottom is with pure water and no soap. If you wish, you can use a non-soap cleanser such as Cetaphil, Moisturel Sensitive Skin Cleanser, or SCF. But the fewer skin-care products you use, the better. One study found that 12 percent of commonly used skin-care products for babies could be considered toxic.[111]

"My daughter is such a joy to be with, even though she's fast approaching 'the twos' and likes to throw herself on the floor screaming for no apparent reason except that I have insensitively chosen the wrong cup for her juice, or the wrong juice for her cup, or whatever."

A rashy bottom will heal quickest if it can breathe. When you can, dress the baby in just a soft cotton diaper or underpants, and leave off waterproof pants. (See the chart "Treating Diaper Rash.")

Your Crying Toddler

As a baby grows into a toddler, he again finds new things to cry about. He may cry from falls and injuries while he is learning to walk, and he may cry from boredom. He may continue to cry from anxiety, as when you leave the room without telling him, or you leave him with a babysitter. Most of all he will cry from frustration—when you won't share the kitchen knife with him, or let him sweep library books off their shelves, or allow him to tear apart his sister's elaborate fantasy world of blocks and dolls.

You may be able to soothe a young toddler with a hug or a few sucks at the breast, or with the old "carrot-on-the-stick" approach, by which you distract him with something else interesting. When he is around eighteen months to two years of age, though, your baby-turned-tot is likely to stand before you screaming "No!" His willfulness can be a shock at first, and a challenge for months to come. Temper tantrums, in which a toddler throws himself to the floor with inconsolable crying, are a normal part of a youngster's newly emerging sense of self. This period in a child's development has been aptly called the "first adolescence."

Sometimes there isn't anything you can do to prevent or minimize a tantrum; it just has to run its course. Screaming back at a child can only make him madder and prolong the outburst. Hold the child if he'll let you; otherwise just stay close by. When the rage wears off, he'll need your comforting.

Having a tantrum is like blowing a fuse; the toddler has no control over his rage and violent feelings. Children can eventually learn, however, to throw tantrums manipulatively. So if your child throws a tantrum because you wouldn't give him a cookie, don't let him have the cookie now. Don't punish him, either. You want to let him know that the tantrum changes nothing between you.

Tantrums tend to occur when a child is overtired, overstimulated, or hungry. A tantrum may signal that it's time to stop playing and settle down for a nap or for a night's sleep. Or your tot may just need some cuddling; try relaxing with him on the living room couch while you listen to music together. Maybe he needs to let off steam and would feel better after a romp outside. If he's hungry but too

TREATING DIAPER RASH

CAUSE	APPEARANCE	TREATMENT
Chafing	Skin is shiny and red but not sore.	Switch to soft cloth diapers or a different brand of disposables.
Prolonged wetness	Skin in the diaper area is first red, then bumps form, followed by white-headed pimples and weeping areas. The rash appears after the baby sleeps in a wet diaper for 10 to 12 hours, and during a cold, sore throat, or ear infection.	Thickly apply protective ointment. Temporarily use ultra-absorbent disposable diapers. In severe cases, a physician may recommend a 1 percent hydrocortisone cream. *(Steroid creams are not recommended; they can affect the baby's own production of cortisone).*
Sensitivity to fabric softener	Tiny red blisters between the belly button and thighs. Rash may also appear on kneecaps, cheeks, and neck.	Don't use liquid fabric softeners, detergents containing softeners, or softener sheets for the dryer.
Yeast infection (*Candida albicans*)	Fiery red, bumpy rash, sometimes with scaly edges. Often worsens during the day.	Avoid plastic pants and cornstarch-based powders. Your doctor can prescribe an anti-yeast cream.
Diarrhea burn	Bright red ring encircles the baby's anus after a bout with diarrhea.	Apply a thin layer of solid vegetable shortening as temporary skin protection. This should be washed off with mild soap and reapplied after each bowel movement.
Acid urine or bowel movement	A bright red, painful scald around the baby's urine hole or on the baby's bottom, due to acidic foods and juices, such as orange juice.	Avoid citrus, tomatoes, and other acidic fruits, and dilute apple juice with water. Be sure your baby is getting sufficient non-acidic fluids. Remove your baby's soiled diaper immediately.
Sensitivity to plastic	Red patches around the baby's waist and encircling his leg and crotch area, where the plastic parts of disposable diapers touch his skin.	Try a different brand of disposable diapers, or change to cloth diapers.
Strep infection	Brilliant red, swollen area around the rectum. There may be small splits in the skin. Often occurs soon after other members of the family have had sore throats.	Immediate treatment with antibiotics is advised. If untreated, the infection may trigger psoriasis (dime-sized patches of raised skin covered with thick, silvery scales) elsewhere on the baby's body.

WHAT'S MAKING YOUR TODDLER CRY

CAUSE	REASONS WHY	WHAT TO DO
Low frustration tolerance	Extremely bright or very active toddlers are likely to be explosive when things don't go right.	As much as possible, keep things that are forbidden to him out of his sight and reach. Provide toys that are appropriate to his stage of development, such as a tricycle propelled by walking instead of a taller pedaled trike. Don't expect him to understand the concept of sharing yet.
Oversensitivity	Some toddlers are easily overwhelmed by strangers, crowds, noise, or angry words.	Accept your toddler as he is. Offer comfort, or remove your child from a situation that is overwhelming. Don't push your oversensitive tot to socialize when he's not ready, or take him on errands when he's tired or hungry.
Physical illness	Irritability is often the first sign that a child is coming down with a cold or other infection. Other causes of irritability are iron-deficiency anemia and allergies.	Keep your toddler home, and keep activities quiet, until he feels better. Consult a doctor if he doesn't improve.
Punitive discipline	When you turn on a toddler in anger, he can't understand why. You just make him anxious and confused.	Accept your child where he is, instead of trying to make him behave as an adult. Prevent conflicts and accidents instead of reacting after they happen. Keep your sense of humor and try to stay friends with your toddler.
Sibling rivalry	A younger child in a family often feels picked on by older ones, who must defend their toys and games against his eager, but destructive, efforts to join. A toddler with a new baby brother or sister feels, rightly, that he has been supplanted.	Reassure each child of your love, and try to spend some time alone with each of them every day. Help older children find ways to protect their things from the toddler without hurting him. Explain the needs of the younger child in a positive way: "He wants to follow you around because he thinks you are special." Accept the need of an older child now and then to act babyish, and be babied.
Situational stress	Just like older children, toddlers go through periods when life is upsetting. It may be because of a new babysitter, a new baby, financial or marital problems, or new fears about being alone in the night.	Give your toddler sympathy and reassurance about whatever is making him anxious. Baby him more than usual. At times like these parents and children need to take more time out to relax and play together.

fussy to let you make dinner, give him a snack while he waits.

If you're planning a vacation or getting ready to move, or if your child is coming down with a cold or flu, he may regress to more babyish behavior. He clings, he turns shy of strangers, he is less adventurous than usual. At these times you don't want to push him toward independence; he needs more affection and protection until he feels more confident.

Don't feel guilty when your cranky toddler makes you want to scream. Parents go through natural stages of separation, too, when they begin to see their children as separate persons, and begin to yearn for more personal freedom. Guilt can make you overcompensate for these yearnings by being too inconsistent or lenient. It's essential, however, to control your anger. Take some deep breaths; leave the room if you must. If you're tempted to hurt your child, get help (see "Resources for Parents").

If your toddler is going through a fussy or hyperactive stage right now, or has periods of almost unbearable whining, trust that your little one will soon outgrow this behavior. Children are continuously growing and changing. This is what makes parenting so very challenging, but also so very rewarding.

CHAPTER TEN

Taking Care of Yourself

"To hell with housework," declares a mother of a colicky baby in Frances Wells Burck's *Babysense*. "It takes all of your energy, mental as well as physical, to help the poor thing through the night."[112]

This mother, like most mothers of less-than-easy babies, has had to confront the "perfect parent" myth that is pervasive in our culture. Magazine ads and television commercials portray the supermom (or sometimes superdad) who presides over an immaculate home, dresses like a model in *Vogue* or *GQ*, sings to a sweet, joyous Gerber baby, and has boundless time and energy to devote to the family. These stereotypes are used ruthlessly to divide the winners from the losers—those who "succeed" from those who "fail" in their parenting roles.

How successful a parent is, according to the myth, is determined by the reactions of her role-complements—her partner and her baby. If a mother feels capable of soothing the fretful infant, then she feels she measures up against society's standards. If the baby continues to cry, then she knows she has failed. If she is able to keep her partner happy, then she has succeeded. If her partner is discontented, then she has failed.

When asked to state who is the most important member of their families, mothers who hold to the perfect-parent myth are more likely *not* to list themselves first. By attempting to conform to the supermom image, many women acquire a tremendous sense of powerlessness, a part of the overall oppression of women, according to the authors of one research study.[113]

Implicit in the myth is the belief that women are responsible for the feelings and behavior of their babies and their partners, and that somehow they are in *control* of all this. If the baby cries, it's your job to stop her. If the baby won't sleep, then it's your task to find a way to *make* her sleep. If your partner is fatigued, jealous, or unhappy about the new baby, then it's your job to placate him. Like the little Dutch boy with his finger in the dike, a mother may find herself overwhelmed by unrealistic expectations for her performance.

Placating and low self-esteem go hand in hand, and they start a vicious cycle. Your baby cries, and you conscientiously try to soothe her. You fail; your baby continues to cry. Your partner gets aroused and angry. You try to make him feel better. You nurse, rock, and jiggle the baby in an effort to try to stop the crying. You fail again. Your baby cries more, your partner withdraws further, and you feel more and more exhausted, lonely, and powerless.

If you're a single mother, the stress of caring for a fussy baby is even greater. You have no one to step in or empathize with you in the night. Your economic situation may require you to return to work quickly, before you feel ready to do so. And this may result in a gnawing sense of guilt and uncertainty because you cannot be with your baby at a time when she seems to need you so badly. You yearn to spend time with old friends and associates, but by the end of the day you're so exhausted from simply trying to cope with work and the baby that you don't feel like going out or having anyone over. Your own need for nurturance gets put on the back burner, somewhere behind caring for the baby, doing the laundry, and putting away the groceries.

Redefining Your Situation

The perfect-parent myth and its illusion of control are not only erroneous but destructive to your emotional well-being and that of your family. At some point you have to realize that it's futile to try to force a baby to go to sleep, or to *make* him not cry—even though baby-training books may try to convince you that you should be in control of these things. Nor can you make a discontented partner feel happy.

Parents who reject the myth of perfection must examine what's really happening to them and redefine their roles on more realistic terms. A couple must come to grips with the fact that they have to stick together through this stressful time, or each will become lost in energy-sapping loneliness.

"On the few occasions that my crying baby fell asleep before I did, I used the time for me. No cleaning, cooking, or washing clothes. I soaked in bubble bath, relaxed with a drink, read a fun book, and prayed that she would sleep a little longer!"

NOTES TO SINGLE PARENTS

✔ Start a telephone list of other single parents and post it on the refrigerator. Bring everyone together for a potluck meal so you can plan a babysitting co-op together.

✔ Schedule one night a week as "My Night Out." Trade off babysitting with another parent. Dress up and go out (even if you feel tired)—shopping, to a singles' gathering, or to a movie or concert.

✔ Seek out opposite-sex singles with children to share outings together (possible sources: Parents Without Partners; personal ads; weekend children's events at museums, theaters, or libraries).

✔ For economy and companionship, consider sharing a house with another single parent and child.

✔ Learn to barter your skills ("I'll babysit for you in exchange for a massage").

✔ Make a list of ways you can make extra cash, such as—catering dinners for friends; caring for someone else's child; selling baked goods to restaurants; producing Saturday morning children's events; buying and selling used clothing, furniture, or toys; creating résumés; grocery shopping for the elderly; teaching a course in your home; pet- and house-sitting.

✔ Always keep a twenty-dollar bill in your wallet so you're never, ever *really* broke.

✔ When you feel blue, give yourself a treat—a rented video, tapes or books from the library, a magazine, a leisurely bath or shower, a bowl of buttered popcorn, an ice cream cone, a hike in the woods, a massage.

✔ Make your bed your castle. Furnish it with plenty of pillows, a warm quilt, floral or flannel sheets—even stuffed animals, if you like.

✔ Focus on the rewards of being single: You can devote yourself to your children without the demands of another adult. You are building your strength and resourcefulness. Remember that it is possible to be very alone while married, and to be very whole and happy while single.

Lena Stefani tells what happened between her and her husband, Chris, this way: "The baby was getting me up over and over in the night. Chris decided that there should be at least one person who got sleep in the night, and that one person would be him. He moved downstairs to the living room couch, leaving me to cope with the baby alone. Without really admitting it, I developed deep resentment toward Chris for abandoning me to deal with our baby all by myself."

Finally, at eleven o'clock one night, when Chris was showered and ready to bed himself down for the night, Lena confronted him with her anger at being stuck with total responsibility for the baby's needs. At first Chris was angry, too. He had missed the touching that had been the mainstay of their affection for each other. He blurted out that he felt like the baby was an unwanted intruder who had shattered an otherwise good marriage.

Lena and Chris tearfully realized that they had to come back together again if they were going to see their way through this crisis. They went into the kitchen, put on a pot of coffee, and sat down to talk about how they could cope better with the baby's needs, and with their need for each other.

"What we concluded that night," Chris remembers, "was that Daniel was not like other babies. He was special. He had special needs. And that meant we were going to have to give him more than other parents probably have to give."

Lena felt she had been forced to be the wellspring—always giving and never receiving. She was able to admit her own hunger to be mothered and fed. Chris admitted his deep desire to be a good father, and his frustration at not knowing how. Holding Lena's hand, he confessed that he really missed her now that the baby took up most of her time.

Miraculously, the baby slept. They tiptoed upstairs to make sure that he was still breathing. He looked so peaceful and pretty lying there. The precious words *I love you* were spoken again. "We love you, too, even if you are a little monster right now," Chris said, gently patting Daniel's diapered bottom. Chris and Lena half-cried and half-laughed. Then they hugged.

The next day Lena woke several times during the night to nurse the baby, but Chris got up once, too, and changed Daniel's diaper. The next day Lena felt happier and more relaxed. Somehow the baby's cries didn't wear her out as they had the day before.

That night Chris fixed dinner while Lena lay on the couch with the baby. While they were eating Chris reached out and squeezed Lena's free hand. Somehow they were going to get through it together.

"Stop blaming yourself for what is going wrong. Redefine your role in a more realistic way. Find things besides baby care that are meaningful to you, even if it's a single daily activity that makes you feel you have some control over your life. It's critical not to adopt the attitude that your needs do not count."

"Our baby had colic the first three months. It's a very frustrating experience for new parents as well as for the baby. There are a whole range of emotions, including anger and guilt. A few times I cried with her out of helplessness. I think parents need to be reassured that these are normal feelings and not to feel bad about them."

That was three years ago. The fussy baby, Daniel, is now a robust, outgoing preschooler. His high energy level still makes him a challenge, but not as much as when he was a baby.

"Chris can't wait to get home to play with Daniel," says Lena. "They've got a very special relationship going." And that's fortunate, because Baby Number Two is due any day. Lena is praying that this baby will be "good," but if she's not, Lena is sure now that she and Chris will manage together somehow.

NOTES TO DAD

✔ Try to get home on time. Things can crumble in those last few minutes that your partner is waiting.

✔ Take the baby away from the house for an hour or two so Mom can nap or take a leisurely bath.

✔ Talk to the baby and say nice things about her. Mom wants to know there is something lovable about her.

✔ Lend a listening ear to your partner. Maybe you can't cure colic, but there is much relief in feeling understood.

✔ Offer to take Mom on an outing. She might say she is too tired, but she needs adult companionship almost as much as sleep.

✔ Make a run for take-out food or cook dinner yourself.

✔ Take over the baby right after dinner or at some other definite time each evening for half an hour or more. (Gentle, quiet touching, talking, and humming work better before bedtime than vigorous play.)

✔ Try letting your baby sleep on your bare chest.

Adapted from D. Bosnos, *CEA Newsletter*, June-July 1980

100 Coping Tips for Parents with Fussy Babies

LAUNDERING AND HOUSEWORK

1. Use a diaper service for six months.
2. Store clothes unfolded on open shelves, or buy five or six laundry baskets to keep sorted but unfolded clean laundry in.
3. When friends ask what they can do to help, schedule them to come in once a week to have tea and do the laundry.
4. Call the high school to find a teenager who can do the heavy housework once a week.
5. Fill the kitchen sink with hot, soapy water in the morning and drop dirty dishes in it for soaking as the day passes, then simply rinse them and let them air-dry. Never towel-dry dishes.
6. To control diaper rash, use 1/2 cup vinegar in the first rinse when washing diapers. The acidity counters bacterial growth.
7. Don't bother to fold clean diapers. Just throw them into a laundry basket beside the baby's changing table or dresser.

FOOD MANAGEMENT

8. To reduce dishwashing, serve food directly from the cooking pan, omit individual plates for finger foods, and keep a supply of paper plates for days when you are exhausted.
9. Buy frozen entrées such as beef stew, lasagna, or fried chicken for emergencies.
10. Prepare dinner in the morning when your energy is high. Make more than enough, and freeze the extra for another dinner later in the week.
11. When you can't make meals ahead, make them quick. Try hamburgers, sandwiches, and foods that can be eaten raw.
12. Stock up on high-energy snacks: protein-rich foods like nuts and cheeses; vitamin-rich foods like dried and fresh fruits, vegetables that can be eaten raw, and juices; and whole-grain crackers.
13. Make your own frozen dinners from leftovers. Include an entrée, vegetables, and fruit on used foil trays or microwave plates. Cover with foil or plastic wrap, and label.
14. Eat like a king for breakfast so you'll have energy for the lows that usually hit around 2:30 to 4:30 in the afternoon.
15. For fast mini-meals, learn how to make nutritious shakes from fruits, yogurt, and other natural ingredients.

"Be good to yourself. Your ego may be wobbly because you are fulfilling someone else's needs twenty-four hours a day. You may find yourself exhausted, obsessed with the baby, and feeling something less than a human being. What you need is mothering yourself."

16. Equip a small playpen or crib with a musical mobile and toys for the baby to watch and play with in the kitchen when you're trying to cook dinner.
17. Go out to eat weekly. Babies usually get a warm welcome at low-budget ethnic restaurants.
18. Start a weekly dinner co-op with other families who have colicky babies. You can all eat and commiserate together.
19. Take daily vitamin B-complex tablets for more energy.

SOOTHING YOUR BABY

20. Buy a used carriage with springs so you can jiggle the baby to sleep anywhere.
21. To help your baby to sleep, tape the noise of the vacuum cleaner, her own voice, or the white noise from a radio station that's off the air.
22. Try letting the baby sleep upright in her car seat or infant seat to ease digestive pains.
23. Keep booties on a fussy baby twenty-four hours a day.
24. Invest in a baby pack or sling and keep the baby in it whenever she's fussy.
25. *Never* wake up a baby to change her diaper.
26. Once the baby's asleep, *don't* move her.
27. Provided it's not too cold outside your front door, briefly stand with your fussing baby in a rush of fresh air.
28. Lay a firm couch cushion on the floor, and put the baby on it to nap with her legs hanging down over the edge. (Use a waterproof pad to protect the cushion.)
29. Don't worry about the baby getting cold during the night. She needs no more covers than you do, and she may prefer none at all.
30. Give your baby sunbaths even in winter by putting her naked in her infant seat or on a quilt in front of a window where sun comes in.
31. To ease belly pains, put the baby belly-down on a warm hot-water bottle on your lap.
32. Give the baby a teaspoon of boiled, cooled water about ten minutes before a feeding if she gets upset when she's hungry.
33. Try different carrying positions to ease the baby's belly pain. Use the "colic carry," with the baby lying face down on your arm, her cheek at your elbow. Or carry her with her back against your belly, pressing her knees up against her stomach.

34. Lay the baby on her right side for a few minutes and then raise her upright to bring up swallowed air.

35. Help the baby to pass gas or move her bowels by putting a small glycerin suppository, or your lubricated pinky finger (nail clipped), into her rectum.

36. Put the baby, wearing only diapers, on Dad's bare chest so they can take a nap together.

37. To stop her from crying, raise the baby as high as you can (while supporting the back of her head), and then lower her almost to the ground with a deep knee bend.

38. Make fennel tea by boiling a tablespoon of fennel seeds in a cup of water. Strain out the seeds, and give the baby a teaspoonful of the tea to ease belly pains.

39. Let the baby sleep on a lambskin. Some parents say their babies will sleep anywhere on their lambies.

40. Sing soothing songs in your deepest voice, putting the baby's name in every so often. (Try "Old Man River" for a start.)

41. Try dance-walking the baby (step-pause, step-pause) while rhythmically groaning your most primitive animal sounds.

42. Stuff your smelliest T-shirt or nightgown next to the baby when she's sleeping so she feels secure when you're not close.

43. If the baby seems to be having teething pains, let her chew on your finger or on a damp, cold washcloth.

DIAPERING AND BATHING

44. Take the baby into a warm bath with you so you can both relax.

45. Bathe the baby in a plastic laundry basket in the tub to reduce the risk of slipping.

46. Change the baby in your lap so she doesn't get chilled and isn't afraid of falling.

47. Sponge-bathe the baby under a warm blanket if she's upset by baths.

48. Cut the baby's fingernails while she sits in your lap, back to you, so that her hands are positioned as yours would be if you were cutting your own nails. If she gets too upset, clip her nails while she's asleep.

49. Don't put Q-Tips or anything else up your baby's nose or into her ears to clean them. They are self-cleaning organs.

50. Double- or triple-diaper the baby at night so wetness won't bother her or you.

51. Let your baby push against your hand with her feet when she's struggling to have a bowel movement.
52. Nail a lightweight bookcase, or install brackets and shelving, at eye-level over the baby's changing table or dresser so that you have *everything*—diapers, cream, cloths—within reach. Or construct a diaper-changing area around the bathroom sink.

REST AND RELAXATION

53. Sleep when the baby does, night or day.
54. Take your older kids to a friend's house so you can have a private rest time with your baby. Or set up a daily quiet time when everyone—you, the baby, and older children—naps, listens to music, or reads.
55. Find a favorite nearby retreat spot—a lake or a meadow, or a private corner of the garden—and go there with the baby every afternoon for an hour.
56. Make the baby a padded bed in a laundry basket, drawer, or sturdy box, so you can carry her around with you from room to room.
57. Turn the bedroom clock to the wall so you won't know when it's 4:30 in the morning.
58. Buy yourself a collection of short novels for reading in the middle of the night.
59. Place a book of inspirational quotations or Bible verses next to the toilet for quick pick-me-ups.
60. Collect pictures—of inspiring artwork, beautiful scenery, or house interiors—for a "dream file" that you can pull out during low moments.
61. Put your favorite sayings on the bathroom mirror, the kitchen cabinet, or anywhere at eye level, so that you see them as you move around the house.
62. Take mini-rests wherever you find yourself with a breather—in the kitchen, under the dining room table, on the living room floor. When the moment presents itself, grab it!
63. Put the baby in a baby pack and walk and walk. The fresh air, exercise, and changing scenery are the best thing in the world for both of you.
64. Get a haircut or a permanent, so that even if you're exhausted you can still feel that you look good.
65. Unplug the phone if you need to sleep.

66. Trick your body into sleeping during the day by taking off your clothes, or even by putting on pajamas and closing the window shades.

67. Don't plan any trips for the first six months after the baby is born. Let your relatives come to you.

68. Send off for baby clothes catalogs and toy catalogs in winter.

69. If you've tried everything to calm your crying baby, then lay her in her bed, take a quick shower, and come back and take a rest, with the baby lying on top of you.

70. Take a "leave of absence" day *with* your baby. Go to a park or a beautiful spot for the day, or simply stay in bed all day, snuggled up next to the baby.

71. Buy a small portable tape player and earphones and play beautiful music to yourself when you're awake in the middle of the night.

72. Have everyone in the family eat a high-protein snack before coming home, and then have a daily rest hour on a quilt on the living room rug instead of the usual dinnertime frenzy.

73. Play the most beautiful music you can find on the stereo during the baby's fussy hours.

74. Take a bath with your partner and baby together to help make up for lost "skin time."

GETTING SUPPORT

75. Start a parent-baby support group with other new parents in the neighborhood. Take turns opening your homes to the group.

76. Trade baby care with another parent—one afternoon a week at your house, another afternoon at hers.

77. When the phone rates are low, call supportive family members, and tell them how much it means to you to talk with them. Ask them to call you at regular times during the week.

78. When relatives ask about your baby's crying, tell them she's under a doctor's care and that you hope to find an answer to her pain within the next few months. (She'll probably outgrow it by then, anyway.)

79. Don't worry what your neighbors think about your baby's crying. If they say anything to you about it, tell them she has a postbirth complication, or some such, and that it's expected to clear up in twelve weeks.

80. Subscribe to parenting publications, such as *Mothering* and La Leche League's *New Beginnings* (see "Recommended Reading"), for supportive, inspirational reading.
81. If Grandma and Grandpa are far away, call the local senior center and ask if an elderly member of the community might be interested in befriending your family.

DECORATING

82. Put a rocking chair and a footstool in the kitchen, if there's room.
83. Install a hammock in the kitchen or the living room with a wall lamp nearby for rocking and reading with the baby.
84. Keep an aquarium in the baby's bedroom for humidity, light, and a soothing droning sound.
85. Use black-out shades or heavy blankets on the windows so the baby won't be awakened by morning light or sounds.
86. Build a changing table by mounting a sturdy plywood slab right into the closet so that it lies flush against all sides.
87. Decorate the baby's diapering area at eye level with small prints, postcards, greeting cards, favorite photos, wise sayings, a small mirror, and other eye-pleasers especially for you.
88. Make a nursing nest with a lot of cushions that can be arranged for your comfort and support. Include a footrest, if you like, and a table for drinks.
89. Get an insulated pitcher, fill it with your favorite iced drink, and put it next to your nursing nest with a glass for refreshments all day.
90. Buy a sausage-shaped bolster, or stuff one yourself, to fit under your nursing arm to ease muscular strain.
91. Place a basket in the bathroom for the daily mail. You can pick out what to read and what to toss out while you're there.
92. Try rearranging your environment for a while. Pull your mattress into the living room and make the bed on the floor. Have a picnic, or play the stereo, and relax for a change!
93. Drag out the old beanbag chair for real relaxation while nursing, but be careful not to leave the baby on it alone (she could suffocate).

MASSAGE

94. When the baby has gas, try giving her a belly massage by gently pressing your fingers around clockwise until the trapped gas is freed (see page 26).

95. If your baby's a biter, it may be because her jaw muscles go into spasms. Try gently massaging her cheek, the temple area, and directly under her chin bone.
96. If your baby arches her back shortly after she nurses, try massaging the back of her neck, her shoulders, and shoulder blades with rotating fingertips. Perhaps she has painfully contracting muscles.

EXERCISE

97. Stretch as dogs and cats do, arching your back and reaching for the ceiling, at least three times a day.
98. Create your own yoga program by slowly stretching, squatting, reaching, and bending to loosen whichever muscles are tight in your own body.
99. Dance to music with your crying baby; she'll probably calm down.

DANGEROUS DON'TS

100. Don't leave balloons within your baby's reach; she could suffocate if one gets into her throat. Watch out for small rattles and pacifiers, often attached to gifts, that can become lodged in a baby's throat. Never tie a baby's pacifier around her neck; this practice has caused death from strangulation. Don't make the baby's bath too hot; water that feels comfortable to you can scald a baby. Don't keep thin plastic dry cleaner's bags; tear them up and throw them away, as they have caused numerous suffocation deaths.

CHAPTER ELEVEN

Overcoming Stress and Depression

BETWEEN HALF AND THREE-QUARTERS of all mothers experience a period of weepiness around the third day after giving birth, about the time the milk comes in.[114] Typically, a mother feels stressed, fatigued, and mildly depressed. These feelings are probably caused by a combination of things—the radical hormonal changes that occur after birth, the physical stress of labor, the emotional experience of giving birth, lack of sleep, and reactions to any drugs administered during labor and delivery. The "baby blues" are unpleasant, but they usually disappear on their own, sometimes just as quickly as they came.

Coping with the Baby Blues

Taking it easy during the first week and a half after you give birth can make an enormous difference in your physical and emotional health months later. You should plan to spend the entire first week, at least, resting with the baby. Dad should plan to take at least a week off from work. If you have older children, a grandparent or babysitter can be a big help in caring for them, and in doing housework, cooking, and shopping. Or you may want to hire a temporary housekeeper or "doula"—a person to mother *you*. You can prepare and freeze meals before the baby is born to make the transition easier, or arrange in advance for friends to bring meals over. Friends and relatives should be asked to keep their visits short unless they are coming to help.

Dealing with Accumulated Stress

Even if you take good care of yourself in the beginning, you'll have a hard time dealing with the stress of a constantly crying, sleepless baby. How much of this stress you can endure depends on a number of things, including your attitude to it, your adaptability, and your general health. But too much constant stress eventually begins to take its toll on any parent's body.

People can usually cope with a relatively high degree of stress for short periods of time. You have an automatic "fight or flight" response—to confront the enemy or run away. Your body gets ready for either feat by releasing hormones into the bloodstream that increase blood supply to the muscles while slowing down digestive processes. You aren't facing a saber-toothed tiger—only a tiny baby whose cries cause your heart to pound and your blood pressure to rise. Yet your body still reacts as it might to the tiger.

When such stress is continuous, your body's natural protective system gets out of balance. It goes into "red alert." At first you find yourself extremely alert and aware. On the outside, you have a smooth veneer of calm, but on the inside, you're contracted. Your muscles are taut. Your mouth feels dry. Your mind races with plans about how you're going to react the next time your baby sounds the alarm. Even though the stress is building up inside you, you may not be totally conscious of it.

Next, numbness and exhaustion set in. You begin to feel weighted down with fatigue. You lack energy for anything but the unending job of responding to your baby's unpredictable cries. Daily tasks that used to be a breeze now loom as huge as mountains before you. It becomes difficult even to bathe, eat, or get the dishes done. You may feel lucky to complete just one task before the day ends and another night of interrupted sleep sets in. You feel terribly disorganized. You find yourself putting the groceries away in the wrong places, forgetting your phone number, or being so preoccupied with the baby's crying that hours pass without your noticing. "My brain just turned into hamburger," one mother recalls, looking back on months of trying to cope with her baby's round-the-clock crying.

Some of the symptoms of prolonged physical and emotional stress are high blood pressure, emotional outbursts, sporadic bouts of illness, failure to fulfill everyday responsibilities, and lapses in memory. You may experience other symptoms, too—unusual pounding of your heart, breathlessness, trembling, perspiring palms, digestive

"I felt so inadequate as a mother. I felt guilty for my feelings of resentment for my baby. I was a real zombie. It hurt me so to see this little baby of mine crying and screaming in so much pain and not to be able to do anything about it except walk the floors with him day and night."

"Verbalize your feelings. Don't keep them boxed in. It's not having bad feelings that's wrong. It's what you do with them that counts. Talking out your feelings helps."

upsets, and frequent urination. You may start to wonder if you've got something seriously wrong with you, like heart disease, cancer, or AIDS.

RECOGNIZING YOUR FEELINGS. In-laws, neighbors, physicians, and most baby care books do a lot to intensify parents' feelings that they are to blame if something is going wrong with their baby. The burden of that blame often makes mothers and fathers hesitant to admit how profound a family crisis they are experiencing.

Acknowledging your feelings about having a difficult baby is an important first step in beginning to cope with your situation. Two-thirds of the new mothers in one survey confessed that their babies' crying had been a major concern over the past four weeks. Some said frankly they were in despair over it. Almost half reported feeling frustrated. Other words and phrases they used were *bothered, nervous, sorry, upset, helpless, wonder what's wrong, irritable, guilty about feelings, heartbroken*, and *don't know what to do*. Some reported they felt hostile, violent, angry, exasperated, underconfident, hurt at first and then indifferent, uptight at first and later resigned, afraid, worried, anxious, concerned, unloving, unattached, terrible, "like killing her," resentful, confused, fed up, and tearful.[115]

In a similar study of fathers of colicky babies, feelings of confusion, anger, isolation, betrayal, helplessness, panic, fear, and dependency were reported. These feelings got worse when the stress of the baby caused the parents' relationship to deteriorate.[116]

Of the hundreds of parents of fussy babies I have interviewed in the past decade, many reported feelings of ambivalence, anger, guilt, and sometimes irrational fear about their situation or their babies. Even with a placid, contented baby, ambivalence about being a parent is normal. But when your baby seems miserable, your uncertainty about being a parent becomes even greater. You may feel a strong drive to escape the baby, but you are also constantly vigilant about him, for fear something may go wrong when you're not looking. It's not unusual to feel an intense surge of love for your baby one minute, only to be swept up the next minute in a jaw-clamping rage when you can't make things better. Sometimes, when you've exhausted all of your resources (especially at 3:00 A.M.), you may secretly wish you could get rid of this baby and start all over again.

A parent has a natural drive to protect her baby when he is endangered, to launch a direct attack on the thing that's causing him to cry. But how can you attack something called colic, or fight an entity called night waking? There's no outlet for your aggression, and this is bound to make you feel angry or frustrated.

You've got to express it somehow. Parents often take out their frustrations about their baby on each other, in arguments and fights. Sometimes parents sit down and cry right along with their babies. Others turn their aggression on themselves, becoming listless and depressed.

Most parents of less-than-easy babies confess that they feel guilty at times. You're afraid you're making mistakes. People have told you pacifiers are bad, but you use them because they're the only thing that will stop your baby from crying. Or you fill a prescription for a drug to make your baby sleep, but you feel so bad about using it that you leave the bottle unopened in the medicine cabinet. Sometimes you feel as if you're constantly walking on eggshells—one wrong step and your baby may be damaged for life.

Fears about the baby and fantasies of escape loom large, especially at night. "Maybe he's retarded, or brain-damaged . . . or maybe he has a fatal illness." You might secretly consider buying an airplane ticket and flying to a far-off city, leaving your baby behind for your husband to discover when he gets home. Fortunately, fears and fantasies like these seldom survive the light of day.

When feelings—ambivalence, guilt, fear, or anger—are harbored inside and not expressed, they can grow until they surround you like walls, leaving you terribly alone. But when you risk expressing your feelings openly to yourself and others, a door opens. You can begin to assess your options rationally, and others can give you support. You start unraveling your tangled emotions, and you begin to recognize how they are compounding your stress. You become increasingly aware of the profound ways your baby is affecting you. Becoming more realistic and truthful about where you are can help you to free up your energies for rebalancing your life.

LEARNING DYNAMIC RELAXATION. If you've built up muscular tension from dealing with your baby, you need to release it. You can do so by consciously relaxing. Dynamic relaxation won't take away the stress of your baby's crying and sleeplessness, but it can help you to feel better and to cope better. You'll discover that even though you may not be able to control your baby's crying, you can have some control over your body's response to it.

Dynamic relaxation brings about immediate changes in your body, including decreased breathing and heart rates. Like sleep, it

"Most parents who harbor some negative feelings cannot bear to face them consciously. They may also be afraid that direct expression of such negative feelings would lead to acts of hostility or aggression. So they repress the feelings instead, and this in turn arouses feelings of guilt."

G. D. JENSEN
The Well Child's Problems

A Self-Help Guide for Parents

Symptom	Description	Self-Treatment
Fatigue	You feel weighted down, tired, drained. Just going up the stairs seems like a burden. While diapers and dirty dishes pile up, you look in the mirror, thinking you may have a dreaded disease.	Do just the minimum housework necessary, or hire someone to come in and help out for a few hours a week. Divide up a dirty room as though it were a clock. Determine where 12:00 is and clean from that spot to 1:00. Then work your way to 2:00. When you get to 3:00, congratulate yourself for having finished one-quarter of the room. Focus on what you have accomplished rather than what is still to be done. Put everything out of your mind except the one thing you are doing at the moment, and then give that one thing your total concentration. You're not sick, you're just exhausted. Sleep when the baby does, even during the day. Take a walk outside at least once a day—rain, snow, or shine. Be sure that you are eating properly. Buy foods that can be prepared quickly and make shakes or other quick pick-me-ups.
Fear	You're afraid something is wrong with the baby, or with yourself. You secretly fear that you're not a good parent. You don't want other parents to know, or your mother-in-law to find out. You blame the problems between you and your baby on the fact that you don't measure up.	Bring your fears out into the open with someone who can help you sort them out. This way you can begin to let go of those that are completely unfounded. With some fears you may need help from outside your circle of family and friends. For example, your doctor can reassure you that your baby is all right, that his crying and sleeplessness will not be harmful to him, and that this behavior will eventually subside. Get a physical exam to make sure that you are healthy. Remind yourself that your mother-in-law is no better at parenting than you are—she's forgotten a lot—and that other parents are secretly feeling the same way you are. They need your companionship and honesty just as you need theirs. Accept the fact that no one feels adequate in the face of an inconsolable baby. Your baby's problems are not because of you. He needs your loving presence, though. Although he can't say thank you his future development will show the influence of your giving.

A SELF-HELP GUIDE FOR PARENTS—*Continued*

SYMPTOM	DESCRIPTION	SELF-TREATMENT
Excessive guilt	You take all the blame for your baby's discomfort. You think you should suffer, too. You worry over not being or doing enough. His crying is your fault. If he gets hurt, it's because you weren't watching. If he gets sick, it's because you let someone who had a germ touch him.	Accept that you're only human. Don't waste your energy with self-blame when you could be enjoying the simple pleasures of everyday living, like the taste of good food and the touch or voice of someone you love. Forgive yourself your shortcomings. Talk over your feelings with other parents who have had fussy babies. Take notice of the times when you do something that fits your image of good parenting. Never miss a chance to congratulate yourself. Allow yourself an hour each day that belongs exclusively to you, even if you stay in the house. Trade off with your spouse, call in a relative, or pay somebody to help out. Get a haircut, buy a book to read in small doses, get a recording you like and dance to it, or go browse at the library.
Nightmares and insomnia	You dream that you, your mate, or your baby is killed in a crash or catastrophe, or that you're being carried away from your baby in an ambulance. Or you find you can't sleep—your brain is racing and you're tossing and turning but you can't fall asleep.	Such a nightmare is a normal sign of stress for parents who are suddenly burdened with more responsibility than they feel they can handle. Immediately counter the dream by imagining yourself as powerful and the outcome as you would want it. Or picture your family together on a tropical island, everyone smiling and happy. Change beds or go to the couch. Use periods of night wakefulness constructively. Send loving prayers to others who could use your blessings. Save a good book just for nighttimes. Read or listen to music. Eat if you're hungry, or drink a soothing herb tea or warm milk. Once you turn night wakings into a positive experience, they cease to be a problem.
Hopelessness	You wake up wishing you could be someplace else. You feel totally unable to control your life—like a hapless victim. It seems there's no exit and there's nothing you can do to change matters. You feel this stage of life will last forever.	Find some small part of your life that you can control. Do one task a day very well. Praise yourself generously for each nice thing you do for yourself, your partner, or your baby. Realize that you are choosing to give.

Continued on next page

A SELF-HELP GUIDE FOR PARENTS—*Continued*

SYMPTOM	DESCRIPTION	SELF-TREATMENT
Hopelessness *(continued)*		Buy yourself a large artist's tablet, and on it list goals for the coming decade of your life. Rather than just wishing for objects, wish for attainments, including the development of good qualities in yourself. Draw symbolic pictures of these attainments, so that you can keep them fresh in your mind. Look forward to the lifelong qualities you hope your baby will develop as he grows. Enroll yourself in an evening course, if only as an observer, to prove you can still absorb information and learn new skills. Cultivate a friendship with another parent and converse every day, if only during a walk around the block or a two-minute telephone call. Buy a book of familiar quotations or inspirational verses and tie it by a string to the toilet paper holder for brief retreats.
Anger	You find yourself blowing up at small irritations. You secretly harbor deep rage toward your baby, or toward your mother or father because they were poor role models. The anger may express itself as oversolicitousness coming through gritted teeth.	Vent explosive feelings toward a sympathetic listener (other than your spouse) to relieve the intensity. Write angry letters (that you tuck away) or keep a journal. You have a right to feel anger, but you shouldn't carry it around like baggage. Dump it and be free of it by finding a safe outlet for physical expression. Beat anger out on the bed or couch with a belt, a bat, a piece of hose, or a tennis racquet. Get it out scouring, scrubbing, pounding dough, flattening meat, hammering nails, yanking weeds, or shoveling. Play golf, softball, squash, tennis, or another sport that demands a smash, wallop, or a fling, or simply run off the energy. Less strenuous forms of exercising, such as walking, dancing, skating, swimming, or bicycle riding, can also vent off steam. Afterward, massage your sore muscles and forgive yourself for feeling angry.

A Self-Help Guide for Parents—*Continued*

Symptom	Description	Self-Treatment
Physical symptoms	Palpitations of your heart, shortness of breath, trembling, nausea, muscle aches, cold sweats, irritability, fits of crying, forgetfulness.	These are all symptoms of stress from the profound life change of giving birth and learning to care for a baby twenty-four hours a day. When the stress eases up, the symptoms go away. Get exercise every day. Tactile experiences can be soothing: bake bread just to knead the dough, or pound and mold clay. Play in the sandbox with the children. Adopt a smooth rock to stroke in your pocket in times of stress until you can collect yourself. Find a natural setting such as a waterfront or a stream, and spend time there with the baby for restoration. Above all, be kind to yourself. After all, you're the only person you really have in life. Mother yourself by getting a massage, taking hot baths, getting rest.

gives your body a rest, only without taking much of your time. People who regularly relax this way claim that it helps in dealing with stress throughout the day (and in the case of parents with fussy babies, throughout the night, too!).

The easiest relaxation techniques are probably the same ones you learned in childbirth preparation classes. First become aware of your tight spots—chronically tense muscles in your body. Anger is often stored in jaw and neck muscles. You may need deep massage in these areas to help them relax. Strumming frozen muscles like the strings on a guitar, or kneading them like bread, can get rid of stiffness and pain.

Pay attention to how groups of muscles in your body operate together and become taut or painful when you're under stress. Pain in the temples is often related to jaw clenching. Headaches often arise from taut muscles in the neck, on either side or at the base of the skull. Stiffness in the shoulders, from carrying the baby, may extend all the way down the arms to the wrists. Stomachaches may be related to tension around the diaphragm or lower abdomen. Check yourself frequently for tension in the places you tend to hold it, and consciously let those muscles relax. Whenever you can put the baby down for a moment, *stretch*.

"The most important thing is to try not to blame yourself."

When you can count on a few minutes' break from your baby, try progressively relaxing different parts of your body while concentrating on a single image in your mind. Follow these steps:

1. Lie quietly on the floor, on the couch, or in bed, in whatever position is most comfortable for you.
2. Close your eyes, and keep them closed.
3. Slowly take three deep breaths. Inhale through your nose as deeply as you can, and then exhale through your mouth as slowly as you can.
4. Breathe normally for about one minute as you picture a place of awesome beauty, such as mountains, a meadow, or a seashore.
5. Take a deep breath, and clench your left hand as tightly as you can.
6. Exhale slowly through your mouth as you hold your hand tightly closed.
7. Slowly unclench the hand and concentrate on the relaxed feeling this gives you.
8. Breathe normally, and concentrate on your beautiful vision for one minute.
9. Take a deep breath, and tighten your right hand, repeating steps 6 through 8. Do the same with other parts of your body, such as your legs, your jaw, and your back.
10. Lie still, breathing normally, for a couple of minutes before getting up.

After some practice in progressive relaxation, try staying calm in the face of stress—that is, in the face of your howling baby. As you go about trying to soothe him, imagine him as smiling and thriving, even though he may seem hopelessly far from that image right now. Picture yourself holding this peaceful baby as you walk through a beautiful meadow. Breathe deeply and relax your muscles as you have done while lying down.

If you suffer from chronic muscular stiffness and pain, you may need regular massages. Maybe your partner can provide them, when the baby goes to sleep, or perhaps you'll want to seek the help of a massage therapist or physical therapist. Loosening up those tight spots and keeping them loose can help you feel better about your body and your baby.

Postpartum Depression

Sometimes a mother experiences a long-term emotional letdown after birth. This is called postpartum depression. She may begin to feel trapped by the responsibility of caring for a small, dependent baby, and she may become "depressed about being depressed." Her emotions may become volatile. She's angry one minute, and crying or withdrawn the next. She has a hard time sleeping. She tosses and turns even after the baby has gone to sleep because she can't seem to shut off her mind and her worries. She may sometimes feel overwhelmed by feelings of anxiety and panic. And she may lose her appetite for a while.

Postpartum depression is really a catch-all term for several kinds of emotional problems that can emerge within the first month or so after childbirth. Approximately 10 percent of all women experience postpartum depression, in varying levels of severity. Women who have experienced emotional problems before their babies were born, such as affective, manic-depressive, or anxiety disorders, are more vulnerable to postpartum depression, and approximately one out of ten mothers who have it also suffered from bouts of depression while they were pregnant.

Two of the more serious forms of postpartum depression are panic disorders and obsessive-compulsive disorders. A mother may be immobilized by fear. She may think that she's going to stop breathing, that she's going to die. Or she may be convinced she can't stay in the same room with the baby because of what she might do to him. She may insist that all the knives be put in the attic because she's afraid of stabbing or hurting the baby. She may be afraid that the baby will be dropped down the stairs, kidnapped in the mall, or hurt in some other way. Some mothers carry secret thoughts of suicide. With any of these disorders, mothers often know within days after birth that something just isn't right. Such feelings are a sure signal to seek professional help.

The precise causes of postpartum depression are not clearly understood. It is known, though, that mothers undergo a rapid loss of estrogen and progesterone after birth, and that this loss may be associated with altered thyroid and cortisol levels. If you're seriously depressed or anxious, you should have your thyroid level checked.

"Try using the deep breathing that you learned in your childbirth classes, while stretching up or bending over and touching your toes. Nurse lying down. Take the phone off the hook. Read a book or magazine. Have your husband rub your back, shoulders, or face. Lie down on the floor with the baby. Just get off your feet."

"Get out of the house and do anything. Literally anything. Get out at least once a day, rain or shine. You don't need to get away from the baby as much as from the dust, the dirty bathroom, the laundry, and the dishes in the sink. Go out with the baby. You need a change of scenery. If you don't get out you'll be tensely sitting there waiting for the baby to wake up from his nap."

FACTORS THAT MAY CONTRIBUTE TO POSTPARTUM DEPRESSION

✔ Your mother, your grandmother, or your aunt has suffered from depression or an affective disorder.

✔ You tend to worry a lot. You are constantly bugged about small things.

✔ You have a bad opinion of yourself. You're afraid you're a bad mother. You feel incompetent. And you may worry that the baby is flawed somehow, too.

✔ You have a compulsive eating or drinking disorder. You are either eating all the time, or not eating at all. Or you find yourself starting to smoke or drink again.

✔ You have to have everything under control. Everything has to be perfect, or you feel overwhelmed with anxiety. You have a lot of "shoulds" in your life, and when you don't live up to them, you get depressed.

✔ You are single with no emotional support, or your marriage is failing.

✔ You are taking birth-control pills.

You may be suffering from thyroiditis or a hypothyroid condition that needs to be treated. This is particularly likely if you've had a thyroid disorder in the past—say, when you were a teenager. Low thyroid levels can also affect milk production, making a breastfed baby fussy and hungry all the time. If this is your problem, taking low-dose thyroid replacement medication may quickly relieve your anxiety and sleeplessness. If a thyroid condition is not the problem, there are other medications that may bring about a positive and rapid change in how you feel.

The Danger of Child Abuse

Child abuse occurs most often among depressed or extremely stressed parents who have very fussy babies. In one study, excessive crying was given as the reason for child abuse by 80 percent of the parents who battered babies under one year of age.[117] Over half the mothers in another survey found that their babies' crying made them feel like battering their babies, and 20 percent reported having hit or shaken their babies in response to the babies' crying.[118]

Particular circumstances that combine to cause child abuse include isolation and loneliness; other stresses in the family, such as unemployment, alcoholism, impending divorce, a recent move to a strange city, or the recent death of a loved one; the parent's own experiences of being abused; and the attitude that violence against children is proper "discipline."

If your baby's crying is wearing you down to the point that you can't bring yourself to comfort him, or you are afraid you might hurt him, then you should seek extra support for yourself right away. See "Resources for Parents," pages 153–55.

"I feel like I'm going to jump out of my skin. I feel like I'm losing my mind. I'd like to get in the car and never come back. I'd like to go to sleep and never wake up. I have thoughts of killing myself."

A MOTHER SUFFERING FROM
POSTPARTUM DEPRESSION

A CLOSING PARABLE

It was the day of the annual baby give-away, when excited couples gathered together to choose the baby that was to be theirs for life.

"I have before me a cherubic, loving baby who makes few demands—a wonderful baby boy," said the auctioneer. "Who will have him?"

"We will!" "We will!" "Give him to us!" mothers- and fathers-to-be shouted. The response was so noisy even the usually quite contented baby began to whimper. The auctioneer banged his gavel for silence.

After much excited talk and negotiation, an eager young couple in the front of the room was awarded the boy. They proudly walked out, carrying him home.

Next came a sweet-looking, smiling baby girl with a tiny pink ribbon in her hair. She was awarded to an older, childless couple in the room who had longed for a child for over a decade.

And so the day went, with babies being presented, then awarded to the couples who seemed the right match for them.

Finally the auctioneer held up a tiny, screaming, red-faced baby. "I have here a little boy who will cry for months after you take him home. You will lose a lot of sleep. He will seem not to appreciate your ministrations, and you will spend many hours of anguish over him. Do I have any bidders?"

No hands went up. In fact, the room became deadly silent. No one wanted to suffer with such a baby. "Ladies and gentlemen," the auctioneer pleaded, leaning over his podium and peering out into the faces of the couples. "Surely someone wants to have this dear, suffering baby?"

People squirmed in their seats and looked at each other, but still no one raised a hand.

"Whoever takes this baby will grow with him," said the auctioneer, who was a wise man. "This baby will break his parents' hearts and then remold them to three times larger than they were before. He will teach his parents how to truly love."

A young couple in the very back of the room rose slowly and walked to the front, hand in hand. "We will take this baby, sir," the father-to-be said, a serious look on his face. He reached out tenderly toward the tiny, crying infant and handed him to his wife.

Their faces were solemn, because they knew they were taking on a hard job. As they walked from the room holding the baby, he hushed for a moment, as though grateful for their stepping forward.

"That couple will be more blessed than all of the others put together," the auctioneer was heard to say as he put away his gavel for the year. "By choosing to love a baby who isn't lovable, they have surely found the path to true compassion."

And so they had.

NOTES

1. D. Sobel, "Baby's Cry Can Speak Volumes," *New York Times*, November 3, 1981.

2. E. C. Rich et al., "The Normal Neonatal Response to Pinprick," *Developmental Medicine and Child Neurology* 16 (1974):432–34; L. Brown, "Physiological Responses to Cutaneous Pain in Neonates," *Neonatal Network* 6 (1987):18–22.

3. Reported by Dr. Gene Cranston Anderson in her lecture "Infants and Mothers as Mutual Caregivers" at La Leche League International's Conference in Miami Beach, July 1991. (An audio tape of the lecture, numbered LL 106–91, is available from Teach 'em, 160 East Illinois, Chicago, Illinois 60611; call 800-225-3775.)

4. National Institute of Mental Health, *Fathers' and Mothers' Responses to Infant Signals: Possible Contributions of Children to Their Own Abuse* (National Institute of Mental Health Research Report RO3-MH-30974), 1979; B. Bleichfeld, "Psychophysiological Responses to an Infant-Produced Auditory Signal: A Comparison of Groups on Women in Different Phases of the Maternal Cycle," *Dissertation Abstracts International* 41, no. 3 (Ann Arbor: University Microfilms, 1980).

5. O. Seitamo and O. Wasz-Höckert, "Early Mother-Child Relationship in the Light of Infant Cry Studies," *Acta Paedopsychiat* 47 (1981):215–22. For other discussions of the effects of crying on breastfeeding mothers see Margaret Mead and Niles Newton, "Cultural Patterning of Perinatal Behavior," in *Childbearing: Its Social and Psychological Aspects*, ed. S. Richardson and A. Guttmacher (Baltimore: Williams and Wilkins, 1967); and V. Vuorenkoski et al., "The Effect of the Cry Stimulus on the Temperature of the Lactating Breast of Primipara: A Thermographic Study," *Experientia* 25 (1969):1286.

6. "Diagnosing Disease from Babies' Cries," *Science Digest*, February 1982, p. 98; "Babies' Cries Aid Diagnosis," *Parents,* October 1979, p. 8.

7. K. K. Berry, "Developmental Study of Recognition of Antecedents of Infant Vocalization," *Perceptual and Motor Skills* 41 (1975):400.

8. D. W. Winnicott, *The Child and the Family: First Relationships* (London: Tavistock, 1957), p. 46.

9. G. Morsbach and C. Bunting, "Maternal Recognition of Their Neonate's Cries," *Developmental Medicine and Child Neurology* 21, no. 2 (1979):178–85.

10. A. Sagi, "Mothers' and Non-Mothers' Identification of Infant Cries," *Infant Behavior and Development* 4, no. 1 (1981):37–40.

11. F. Rebelsky and R. Black, "Crying in Infancy," *Journal of Genetic Psychology* 121 (1972):49–57; T. Berry Brazelton, "Crying in Infancy," *Paediatrics* 29 (1962):597.

12. D. S. Vorster, "Crying and Non-Crying Babies," *British Medical Journal*, 5 July 1980, pp. 58–59.

13. For a thoughtful observation regarding crying and its significance in young hospital patients, see Alice C. Nelson, "How Can You Stand the Crying?" *American Journal of Nursing*, January 1970, pp. 66–69.

14. On studies in the fear of spoiling and its effects on parent-infant relationships, see C. F. Z. Boukydis and R. Burges, "Adult Psychological Response to Infant Cries: Effects of Temperament of Infant, Parental Status and Gender," *Child Development* 53 (1982):704–13; M. L. Lounsbury and J. E. Bates, "The Cries of Infants of Differing Levels of Perceived Temperamental Difficultness: Acoustic Properties and Effects on Listeners, *Child Development* 53 (1982):677–86; S. B. Campbell, "Mother-Infant Interaction as a Function of Maternal Rating of Temperament," *Child Psychiatry and Human Development* 110 (1979):67–76; and J. Milliones, "Relationship between Perceived Child Temperament and Maternal Behaviors," *Child Development* 49 (1978):1255–57.

15. D. Sobel, "Babies' Cry Can Speak Volumes," *New York Times*, 3 November 1981. See also S. B. Crockenberg and K. McCluskey, "Change in Maternal Behavior during the Baby's First Year of Life," *Child Development* 57, no. 3 (1986):746–53.

16. E. B. Thoman, "How a Rejecting Baby Affects Mother-Infant Synchrony," in *Parent-Infant Interaction*, Ciba Foundation Symposium 33, 1975, pp. 185–86.

17. M. D. S. Ainsworth and M. C. Blehar, "Developmental Changes in Behavior of Infants and Their Mothers Relevant to Close Bodily Contact," paper read at the biennial meeting of the Society for Research in Child Development, April 1975.

18. Charles A. Aldrich and Mary M. Aldrich, *Babies are Human Beings* (New York: Macmillan, 1954), pp. 113–14.

19. B. Lozoff and G. Britten, "Infant Care: Cache or Carry?" *American Journal of Pediatrics* 95, no. 3 (1979):478–83.

20. For a discussion of baby product safety, see Sandy Jones and Werner Freitag, *Consumer Reports Guide to Baby Products*, 3rd ed. (New York: Consumer Reports Books, 1991).

21. Sheila Kitzinger, *The Crying Baby: Why Babies Cry, How Parents Feel, What You Can Do about It* (New York: Viking-Penguin, 1989), p. 224.

22. Mary Ann Dzik, "Comforting of the Distressed Infant," *Maternal-Child Nursing Journal* 8, no. 3 (1979):167.

23. D. R. Pederson, "The Soothing Effect of Rocking as Determined by the Direction and Frequency of Movement," *Canadian Journal of Behavioral Sciences* 7, no. 3 (1975):237–43.

24. U. A. Hunziker and R. G. Barr, *Pediatrics* 77, no. 5 (1986):641–48.

25. Susan Goodman, "Presumed Innocents: Newborns: What Do They Know and When Do They Know It?" *Modern Maturity,* December 1991–January 1992, pp. 26–27.

26. In S. Trotter and E. B. Thoman, eds., *Social Responsiveness of Infants,* Pediatric Round Table 2 (Johnson and Johnson, 1978), p. 1.

27. Goodman, "Presumed Innocents."

28. Goodman, "Presumed Innocents."

29. Goodman, "Presumed Innocents."

30. William Sears, *The Fussy Baby: How to Bring Out the Best in Your High-Need Child* (Franklin Park, Ill.: La Leche League, 1985).

31. N. Klougart et al., "Infantile Colic Treated by Chiropractors: A Prospective Study of 316 Cases," *Journal of Manipulative Physiological Therapy* 12, no. 4 (1989):281–88.

32. T. Berry Brazelton, "No One Likes to Hear a Baby Cry," *Redbook,* April 1978, p. 257.

33. Mama Ruby Wright, *Old-Fashioned Baby Care: A Parent's Guide to Burping, Bathing, Feeding, Changing, Playing with and Loving Your New Baby* (New York: Prentice-Hall, 1988), pp. 79–80.

34. *Parents,* October 1970, p. 62.

35. C. M. Johnson, "Infant and Toddler Sleep: A Telephone Survey of Parents in One Community," *Developmental and Behavioral Pediatrics* 12, no. 2 (1991):108–14.

36. M. B. Sterman and Toke Hoppenbrouwers, "Development of Sleep-Waking and Rest-Activity Patterns from Fetus to Adult in Man," in B. Sterman et al., eds., *Brain Development and Behavior* (New York: Academic Press, 1971), pp. 203–27.

37. M. A. Keener, C. H. Zeanah, and T. F. Anders, "Infant Temperament, Sleep Organization, and Nighttime Parental Interventions," *Pediatrics* 81, no. 6 (1988):762–71.

38. R. N. Emde and J. Robinson, "The First Two Months: Recent Research in Developmental Psychobiology and the Changing View of the Newborn," in *Basic Handbook of Child Psychiatry*, ed. J. Noshpitz (New York: Basic Books, 1979), 1:72–105.

39. G. Spangler, "The Emergence of Adrenocortical Circadian Function in Newborns and Infants and Its Relationship to Sleep, Feeding and Maternal Adrenocortical Activity," *Early Human Development* 25 (1991), pp. 197–208.

40. William Sears, *Nighttime Parenting: How to Get Your Baby and Child to Sleep* (Franklin Park, Ill.: La Leche League, 1985), p. 110.

41. Sears, *Nighttime Parenting,* p. 113.

42. J. F. Bernal, "Night Waking in Infants during the First 14 Months," *Developmental Medicine and Child Neurology* 15 (1973):760–69.

43. T. F. Anders and M. Keener, "Developmental Course of Nighttime Sleep-Wake Patterns in Full-Term and Premature Infants during the First Year of Life," *Sleep* 8 (1985):173–92.

44. M. Reite and R. A. Short, "Nocturnal Sleep in Separated Monkey Infants," *Archives of General Psychiatry* 35 (1978):1247–53.

45. Quoted in A. Bass, "Should Newborns Sleep Alone?" *Boston Globe,* March 18, 1988.

46. Quoted in Ruth Winter, "Good Night, Sleep Tight, Please," *Parents,* December 1978, pp. 57–58.

47. For a review of studies on the effects of motion and touching on infantile development see Sandy Jones, *To Love a Baby* (Boston: Houghton Mifflin, 1981), pp. 120–55.

48. Bass, "Should Newborns Sleep Alone?"

49. La Leche League International pamphlet #20 (Franklin Park, Ill.: La Leche League, 1991), p. 5.

50. J. Mercer and R. Russ, "Variables Affecting Time between Childbirth and the Establishment of Lactation," *Journal of General Psychology* 102, no. 1 (1980):155–56.

51. Los Angeles County branch, University of Southern California Medical Center.

52. Ina May Gaskin, *Spiritual Midwifery* (Summertown, Tenn.: Book Publishing Co., 1978), p. 251.

53. Quoted in S. Quinn, "The Competence of Babies," *Atlantic Monthly,* January 1982, p. 59.

54. Gaskin, *Spiritual Midwifery.*

55. M. Ozturk and O. M. Ozturk, "Thumbsucking and Falling Asleep," *British Journal of Medical Psychology* 50 (1977):95–103.

56. Philip O. Anderson, "The Safety of Drugs during Breastfeeding," Appendix B, (Boston: Harvard Common Press, 1990), pp. 191–208.

57. "Drugs in Lactating Women," *Obstetrics and Gynecology Annual* 10 (1981): p. 107.

58. For practical suggestions about bottle feeding see Wright, *Old-Fashioned Baby Care,* pp. 51–70. For detailed advice about choosing bottles, nipples, and other baby feeding equipment, see Jones and Freitag, *Consumer Reports Guide to Baby Products.*

59. R. W. Shepherd et al., "Gastroesophageal Reflux in Children: Clinical Profile, Course and Outcome with Active Therapy in 126 Cases," *Clinical Pediatrics* 26, no. 2:55–60.

60. Keener, Zeanah, and Anders, "Infant Temperament, Sleep Organization, and Nighttime Parental Interventions," pp. 762–71.

61. Richard Ferber, *Solve Your Child's Sleep Problems* (New York: Simon and Schuster, 1985), pp. 75–76.

62. Ferber, *Solve Your Child's Sleep Problems*, p. 81.

63. Ferber, *Solve Your Child's Sleep Problems*, p. 85–86.

64. V. I. Reickert and C. M. Johnson, "Reducing Nocturnal Awakening and Crying Episodes in Infants and Young Children: A Comparison between Scheduled Awakenings and Systematic Ignoring," *Pediatrics* 81, no. 2 (1988):208.

65. K. G. France and S. M. Hudson, "Behavior Management of Infant Sleep Disturbance, *Journal of Applied Behavior Analysis* 23 (1990):91–98.

66. This section is drawn from my interviews with hundreds of parents; a talk with Magda Gerber, a well-known baby care teacher in Los Angeles; and the writings of Nina R. Lief and Mama Ruby Wright. Nina Lief is a specialist in child psychiatry and director of the Early Childhood Development Center at New York Medical College. She is author, with M. E. Fahs, of *The First Year of Life: A Curriculum for Parenting Education* (New York: Keyway, 1979). Ruby Wright *(Old-Fashioned Baby Care)* is a professional baby nurse in New York who has cared for over one thousand newborns.

67. Wright, *Old-Fashioned Baby Care*, p. 77.

68. Wessel et al., "Paroxysmal Fussing in Infancy," *Pediatrics* 14 (1954):421.

69. Marc Weissbluth, *Crybabies: Coping with Colic* (New York: Berkley, 1984).

70. Wessel et al., "Paroxysmal Fussing in Infancy," pp. 421–34.

71. Michael Woolridge, "Colic, Overfeeding and Symptoms of Lactose Malabsorption: A Possible Artifact of Feeding Management," lecture presented at La Leche League International's Physicians' Seminar, July 1991. (An audio tape is available from Convention Tapes International, P.O. Box 381992, Miami, Florida 33238–1992; telephone 305-757-8666).

72. Emelyn L. Coolidge, *Home Care of Sick Children* (New York: D. Appleton, 1916), pp. 134–35.

73. Woolridge, "Colic, Overfeeding and Symptoms of Lactose Malabsorption."

74. Sigvard Jorup, "Colonic Hyperperistalsis in Neurolabile Infants," *Acta Paediatrica Scandinavica* (Supplement) 85 (1952):1–10.

75. R. L. Clark, F. M. Ganis, and W. L. Bradford, "A Study of the Possible Relationship of Progesterone to Colic," *Pediatrics* 31 (1963):65–71; and Marc Weissbluth and O. C. Green, "Plasma Progesterone Concentrations in Infants: Relation to Infantile Colic," *Journal of Pediatrics* 103 (1983):935–36.

76. L. Lothe et al., "Motilin and Infantile Colic: A Prospective Study," *Acta Paediatrica Scandinavica* 79, no. 4 (1990):410–16; and L. Lothe et al., "Motilin, Vasoactive Intestinal Peptide and Gastrin in Infantile Colic," *Acta Paediatrica Scandinavica* 76, no. 2 (1987):316–20.

77. A. Korner et al., "Relation between Prenatal Maternal Blood Pressure and Infant Irritability," *Early Human Development* 4, no. 1 (1980):35–39.

78. D. B. Thomas, "Infant Colic and Drugs in Labour," *Lancet,* February 28, 1981, p. 493; D. B. Thomas, "Infantile Colic—An Iatrogenic Condition," *Australian Paediatric Journal* 17 (1981):130–31; D. B. Thomas, "Aetiological Associations in Infantile Colic: An Hypothesis," *Australian Paediatric Journal* 17 (1981):292–95; and A. D. Murray et al., "Effects of Epidural Anesthesia on Newborns and Their Mothers," *Child Development* 52 (1981):71–82.

79. B. M. Lester et al., "Neurobehavioral Syndromes in Cocaine-Exposed Newborn Infants," *Child Development* 62 (1991):694–705.

80. G. Said, E. Patois, and J. Lellouch, "Infantile Colic and Parental Smoking," *British Medical Journal* 289 (1984):660.

81. Jorup, "Colonic Hyperperistalsis in Neurolabile Infants."

82. Personal interview.

83. Ronald Illingworth, *The Normal Child: Some Problems of the Early Years and Their Treatment* (London: Churchill, 1979), p. 29.

84. For more information on what colic and excessive crying do to parents, see T. Berry Brazelton, "Crying in Infancy," *Pediatrics* 29 (1962):579–88; E. Smith, "To Cry or Not to Cry," *Nursing Mirror* 153 (1981):20–23; S. Menahem, "The Crying Baby—Why Colic?" *Australian Family Physician* 7 (1978):1262–66; W. H. Waldman and D. Salsgard, "Helping Parents Cope with Colic," *Pediatric Basics* 33 (1983):12–14; L. Swaffield, "Cry Babies," *Nursing Times* 80 (1984):16–17; and P. E. Thompson et al., "Effects of Infant Colic on the Family: Implications for Practice," *Issues in Comprehensive Pediatric Nursing* 9 (1986):273–85.

85. S. B. Campbell, "Mother-Infant Interaction as a Function of Maternal Rating of Temperament," *Child Psychiatry and Human Development* 110 (1979):67–76.

86. R. Bell et al., "Organization of Behavior and Relations between Periods," *Monographs of the Society for Research in Child Development* 36 (1971):1.

87. W. B. Carey and S. C. McDevitt, "Stability and Change in Individual Temperament Diagnoses from Infancy to Early Childhood," *Journal of the American Academy of Child Psychiatry* 17 (1978):331–37.

88. D. W. Hide and B. M. Guyer, "Prevalence of Infant Colic," *Archives of Disease in Childhood* 106 (1982):559–60.

89. D. M. Robertson, "Seeds of Later Infant Obesity" (letter), *British Medical Journal*, February 2, 1974, p. 200.

90. A. Kahn et al., "Insomnia and Cow's Milk Allergy in Infants," *Pediatrics* 76 (1985):880–84.

91. Michael A. Schmidt, *Childhood Ear Infections: What Every Parent and Physician Should Know about Prevention, Home Care, and Alternative Treatment* (Berkeley: North Atlantic, 1990), p. 10.

92. Schmidt, *Childhood Ear Infections*, pp. 57–58.

93. Schmidt, *Childhood Ear Infections*, p. 62.

94. B. W. C. Forsyth, P. L. McCarthy, and J. M. Leventhal, *Journal of Pediatrics* 106, no. 6 (1985):1012–17; R. K. Chandra, G. Singh, and B. Shridhara, "Effect of Feeding Whey Hydrolysate, Soy and Conventional Cow Milk Formulas on Incidence of Atopic Disease in High Risk Infants," *Annals of Allergy* 63, no. 2 (1989):102–6; and R. J. Merritt et al., "Whey Protein Hydrolysate Formula for Infants with Gastrointestinal Intolerance to Cow Milk and Soy Protein in Infant Formulas," *Journal of Pediatric Gastroenterological Nutrition* 11, no. 1 (1990):78–82.

95. I. Jakobsson and T. Lindberg, "Cow's Milk Proteins Cause Infantile Colic in Breastfed Infants: A Double-Blind Crossover Study," *Pediatrics* 71 (1983):268–71; and L. Lothe, T. Lindberg, and I. Jakobsson, "Cow's Milk Formula as a Cause of Infantile Colic: A Double-Blind Crossover Study," *Pediatrics* 70 (1982):7–10.

96. Schmidt, *Childhood Ear Infections*, p. 203.

97. The research of Patrick Clyne and Anthony Kulczyski, of the Washington University School of Medicine in St. Louis, reported in "Colic Relief," *Parenting,* September 1991, p. 19.

98. Robert S. Mendelsohn, *How to Raise a Healthy Child . . . in Spite of Your Doctor* (Chicago: Contemporary Books, 1984), p. 69.

99. I. C. Radde and S. M. MacLeod, "Therapeutic and Nontherapeutic Research in Children," in *Textbook of Pediatric Clinical Pharmacology*, ed. S. M. MacLeod and I. C. Radde (Littleton, Massachusetts: PSG, 1985), pp. 435–39.

100. J. Williams and R. Watkins-Jones, "Dicyclomine: Worrying Symptoms Associated with Use in Some Small Babies," *British Medical Journal* 288 (1984):901; and B. Randall, G. Gerry, and F. Rance, "Dicyclomine in the Sudden Infant Death Syndrome (SIDS): A Cause of Death or an Incidental Finding?" *Journal of Forensic Science* 31, no. 4 (1986):1460–74; "Bentyl," *Physician's Desk Reference* (Medical Economics Data, 1991).

101. Morris Green and Julius B. Richmond, "Etiologic Classification of Irritability," in *Pediatric Diagnosis* (Philadelphia: W. B. Saunders, 1980), p. 379.

102. A. Kahn and D. Blum, "Phenothiazines and Sudden Infant Death Syndrome," *Pediatrics* 70 (1982):75–78; R. A. Hardoin et al., "Colic Medication and Apparent Life-Threatening Events," *Clinical Pediatrics* 30, no. 5 (1991):281–85; Erwin Kestrup and Bernie Olan, *Drug Facts and Comparisons—Information* (St. Louis: J. B. Lippincott, 1990), p. 1376.

103. Johnson, "Infant and Toddler Sleep," pp. 108–14.

104. Mendelsohn, *How to Raise a Healthy Child*, p. 210.

105. Randall Neustaedter, *The Immunization Decision: A Guide for Parents* (Berkeley: North Atlantic Books, 1990), p. 6.

106. Schmidt, *Childhood Ear Infections*, p. 3.

107. Schmidt, *Childhood Ear Infections*, pp. 21–28.

108. Schmidt, *Childhood Ear Infections*, pp. 28–31.

109. Schmidt, *Childhood Ear Infections*, p. 31.

110. Schmidt, *Childhood Ear Infections*, pp. 41–42.

111. F. Cetta, G. H. Lambert, and S. P. Ros, "Newborn Chemical Exposure from Over-the-Counter Skin Care Products, *Clinical Pediatrics* 30, no. 5 (1991):266–69.

112. Frances Wells Burck, *Babysense: A Supportive Guide to Baby Care* (New York: St. Martin's, 1979), p. 80.

113. M. C. Lovel and D. L. Fiorino, "Combatting Myth: A Conceptual Framework for Analyzing the Stress of Motherhood," *Advances in Nursing Science*, July 1979, pp. 75–84.

114. *Feelings After Birth: Postpartum Adjustment* (Morrisville, Pennsylvania: Depression after Delivery, 1991), p. 3.

115. J. Harris, "When Babies Cry," *Canadian Nurse* 75, no. 2 (1979):32–34.

116. J. W. Driscoll, "Postpartum Depression: Definition and Management," lecture presented at La Leche League's Thirty-Fifth Anniversary Conference, July 1991. (An audio tape is available from Teach' em, 160 East Illinois, Chicago, Illinois 60611; call 800-225-3775.)

117. *Feelings after Birth*, p. 3.

118. J. Weston, "The Psychology of Child Abuse," in *Sleep and Its Disorders in Children*, ed. R. Helfer and C. L. Kempe (Chicago: University of Chicago Press, 1968), pp. 74–86.

RESOURCES FOR PARENTS

Many cities have drop-in centers where parents can find support through classes, informal counseling, group meetings, discussions on childrearing topics, and family-centered activities. College departments in early childhood education or family studies sometimes offer parenting classes or support groups, and so do some Head Start centers, hospitals, birth centers, childbirth education organizations, churches, and chapters of the YMCA and YWCA. Hospitals and social service organizations sometimes sponsor telephone "warmlines" for parenting information and support.

Counseling is available from publicly funded mental health centers, at little or no cost, and from private family service agencies, which often have sliding fee scales. Churches and synagogues also offer counseling.

A senior center in your community may be able to aid you in finding an elderly person to volunteer as a foster grandparent to your family, and to visit weekly or biweekly.

For help in locating services within your community, consult the Yellow Pages or the reference desk of your public library. Or pick up one of the parenting newspapers that are published in many cities. These papers usually run announcements about children's activities and parents' support groups as well as advertisements for businesses that cater to families. Childbirth education organizations can also be a great help in locating services for parents and children.

The following national organizations can refer you to local services or help you directly:

Childbirth Education Organizations

American Academy of Husband-Coached Childbirth
P.O. Box 5224
Sherman Oaks, California 91413
818-788-6662

ASPO/Lamaze
1101 Connecticut Avenue N.W., Suite 700
Washington, DC 20036
800-368-4404

Childbirth without Pain Education Association
20134 Snowden
Detroit, Michigan 48235
313-341-3816

International Childbirth Education Association
P.O. Box 20048
Minneapolis, Minnesota 55420
612-854-8660

Childhelp U.S.A.
800-422-4453

Call toll-free for crisis counseling, referrals, and literature on child abuse and prevention.

Depression after Delivery
P.O. Box 1282
Morrisville, Pennsylvania 19067
215-295-3994

This organization offers literature on postpartum depression, a list of telephone contacts for depressed new mothers, and local support groups for both mothers and fathers. Send a stamped, self-addressed envelope for written information.

Family Resources Coalition
200 South Michigan, Suite 1520
Chicago, Illinois 60604
312-341-9361

This coalition is compiling a national directory of family support services.

La Leche League International
9616 Minneapolis Avenue
Franklin Park, Illinois 60131
800-LA LECHE

La Leche chapters offer telephone guidance and support groups for breastfeeding mothers (some cities have couples' groups, too). The national office provides literature on breastfeeding and childrearing as well as help in finding a local group.

National Mental Health Association
1021 Prince Street
Alexandria, Virginia 22314
703-684-7722

This organization can provide a referral to one of over six hundred local mental health associations.

Nursing Mothers Counsel
P.O. Box 50063
Palo Alto, California 94303
415-591-6688

Nursing Mothers Counsel offers breastfeeding support through chapters in various cities in California and in Denver, Fort Wayne, and Atlanta. Call for a local number.

Parenting Newspapers
12715 Path Finder Lane
San Antonio, Texas 78230
512-492-9057

Contact this organization to find out where parenting papers are published in your state.

Parents Anonymous
800-421-0353

Call toll-free for a referral to a local Parents Anonymous chapter. The local chapter may offer a telephone hotline or a support group for parents who have abused or are afraid they might abuse their children.

Parents Without Partners
8807 Colesville Road
Silver Spring, Maryland 20910
800-637-7974

An organization of mutual support groups, Parents Without Partners offers educational and social activities for single parents and their children. Call toll-free for a referral to a local group.

RECOMMENDED READING

Compleat Mother. Box 399, Mildmay, Ontario N0G 2J0 Canada.

A newsprint magazine full of information and personal stories on alternative mothering.

Huggins, Kathleen. *The Nursing Mother's Companion*, rev ed. Boston: Harvard Common Press, 1990.

A complete guide to solving breastfeeding problems throughout the first year and beyond.

Jones, Sandy, and Werner Freitag. *Consumer Reports Guide to Baby Products*, 3rd ed. New York: Warner Books, 1991.

Advice on choosing safe, sturdy, and well-priced baby products of every sort.

Liedloff, Jean. *The Continuum Concept.* Reading, Mass.: Addison-Wesley, 1986.

A classic look at the virtues of keeping a baby close to the mother's body, as this is practiced by Amazonian Indians.

Mendelsohn, Robert S. *How to Raise a Healthy Child . . . in Spite of Your Doctor.* Chicago: Contemporary Books, 1984.

A common-sense guide to treating children's illnesses at home, and avoiding overtreatment by physicians.

Mohrbacher, Nancy, and Julie Stock. *The Breastfeeding Answer Book.* Franklin Park, Ill.: La Leche League, 1991.

A comprehensive guide written for La Leche leaders, this book must be ordered directly from La Leche League International, 9616 Minneapolis Avenue, Franklin Park, Illinois 60131. Call toll-free 800-LA LECHE.

Mothering. P.O. Box 1690, Santa Fe, New Mexico 87504.

An attractive and popular alternative parenting magazine.

Neustaedter, Randall. *The Immunization Decision: A Guide for Parents.* Berkeley: North Atlantic Books, 1990.

A well-researched, critical look at vaccinations by a homeopathic physician.

New Beginnings. Franklin Park, Illinois: La Leche League.

An inspiring magazine for breastfeeding mothers, available from La Leche League International, 9616 Minneapolis Avenue, Franklin Park, Illinois 60131. Call toll-free 800-LA LECHE.

Rapp, Doris J. *Is This Your Child?: Discovering and Treating Unrecognized Allergies.* New York: William Morrow, 1991.

A comprehensive guide to the diagnosis and treatment of food and nonfood allergies.

Schmidt, Michael A. *Childhood Ear Infections: What Every Parent and Physician Should Know about Prevention, Home Care, and Alternative Treatment.* Berkeley: North Atlantic Books, 1990.

A thorough, holistic guide by a man trained in chiropractic, acupuncture, nutrition, and homeopathy.

Schneider, Vimala. *Infant Massage: A Handbook for Loving Parents.* New York: Bantam, 1989.

A massage program to enhance infant development and the parent-baby relationship.

Thevenin, Tine. *The Family Bed: An Age Old Concept in Child Rearing,* rev. ed. Garden City Park, New York: Avery, 1987.

The classic guide to shared sleeping.

Wright, Mama Ruby. *Old-Fashioned Baby Care: A Parent's Guide to Burping, Bathing, Feeding, Changing, Playing with and Loving Your New Baby.* New York: Prentice-Hall, 1988.

Practical advice from a long-time baby nurse.

INDEX